Vitus Bering

The Discoverer of Bering Strait

PETER LAURIDSEN

CAMBRIDGE
UNIVERSITY PRESS

CAMBRIDGE UNIVERSITY PRESS

Cambridge, New York, Melbourne, Madrid, Cape Town,
Singapore, São Paolo, Delhi, Tokyo, Mexico City

Published in the United States of America by Cambridge University Press, New York

www.cambridge.org
Information on this title: www.cambridge.org/9781108041515

© in this compilation Cambridge University Press 2012

This edition first published 1889
This digitally printed version 2012

ISBN 978-1-108-04151-5 Paperback

CAMBRIDGE LIBRARY COLLECTION

Books of enduring scholarly value

Travel and Exploration

The history of travel writing dates back to the Bible, Caesar, the Vikings and the Crusaders, and its many themes include war, trade, science and recreation. Explorers from Columbus to Cook charted lands not previously visited by Western travellers, and were followed by merchants, missionaries, and colonists, who wrote accounts of their experiences. The development of steam power in the nineteenth century provided opportunities for increasing numbers of 'ordinary' people to travel further, more economically, and more safely, and resulted in great enthusiasm for travel writing among the reading public. Works included in this series range from first-hand descriptions of previously unrecorded places, to literary accounts of the strange habits of foreigners, to examples of the burgeoning numbers of guidebooks produced to satisfy the needs of a new kind of traveller - the tourist.

Vitus Bering

Vitus Bering (1681–1741) was a Danish-born Russian navigator. He enlisted in the Russian navy and fought during the Great Northern War (1700–21) against the Swedish Empire. In 1725 he received a commission from Peter the Great to discover whether there was a land bridge between Russia and America. He sailed through what would later be called the Bering Strait, but was unable to reach America on this first attempt. He succeeded on his next voyage, later named the Great Northern Expedition, and set about mapping significant sections of North American coastline. He also charted the Arctic coast of Siberia, 'discovered' Japan from the North and became the first European to explore Alaska. Published in English translation for the American market in 1889, this sympathetic biography by the historian and geographer Peter Lauridsen (1846–1923) had originally appeared in Danish in 1885. It includes extensive notes and an index.

Cambridge University Press has long been a pioneer in the reissuing of out-of-print titles from its own backlist, producing digital reprints of books that are still sought after by scholars and students but could not be reprinted economically using traditional technology. The Cambridge Library Collection extends this activity to a wider range of books which are still of importance to researchers and professionals, either for the source material they contain, or as landmarks in the history of their academic discipline.

Drawing from the world-renowned collections in the Cambridge University Library, and guided by the advice of experts in each subject area, Cambridge University Press is using state-of-the-art scanning machines in its own Printing House to capture the content of each book selected for inclusion. The files are processed to give a consistently clear, crisp image, and the books finished to the high quality standard for which the Press is recognised around the world. The latest print-on-demand technology ensures that the books will remain available indefinitely, and that orders for single or multiple copies can quickly be supplied.

The Cambridge Library Collection brings back to life books of enduring scholarly value (including out-of-copyright works originally issued by other publishers) across a wide range of disciplines in the humanities and social sciences and in science and technology.

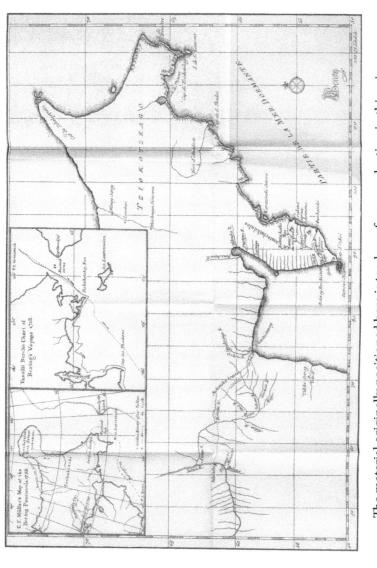

The material originally positioned here is too large for reproduction in this reissue.
A PDF can be downloaded from the web address given on page iv
of this book, by clicking on 'Resources Available'.

RUSSIAN EXPLORATIONS, 1725-1743.

VITUS BERING:

THE DISCOVERER OF BERING STRAIT.

BY

PETER LAURIDSEN,

MEMBER OF THE COUNCIL OF THE ROYAL DANISH GEOGRAPHICAL SOCIETY,
EDITOR OF JENS MUNK'S "NAVIGATIO SEPTENTRIONALIS."

REVISED BY THE AUTHOR, AND TRANSLATED FROM THE DANISH BY

JULIUS E. OLSON,

ASSISTANT PROFESSOR OF SCANDINAVIAN LANGUAGES IN THE UNIVERSITY OF WISCONSIN.

WITH AN INTRODUCTION TO THE AMERICAN EDITION BY

FREDERICK SCHWATKA,

MEDALLIST OF THE PARIS GEOGRAPHICAL SOCIETY, AND OF THE IMPERIAL GEOGRAPHICAL
SOCIETY OF RUSSIA; HONORARY MEMBER OF THE BREMEN GEOGRAPHICAL SOCIETY,
AND THE SWISS GEOGRAPHICAL SOCIETY OF GENEVA; CORRESPONDING MEMBER
OF THE ITALIAN GEOGRAPHICAL SOCIETY, ETC., ETC.; AUTHOR OF
"ALONG ALASKA'S GREAT RIVER," ETC., ETC.

CHICAGO:
S. C. GRIGGS & COMPANY,
1889.

PRESS OF
KNIGHT & LEONARD CO.
CHICAGO.

CONTENTS.

PART II.

THE GREAT NORTHERN EXPEDITION.

PART III.

THE VARIOUS EXPEDITIONS.

CHAPTER XII.

CHAPTER XIII.

CHAPTER XIV.

CHAPTER XV.

CHAPTER XVI.

CHAPTER XVII.

CHAPTER XVIII.

CHAPTER XIX.

APPENDIX.

MAPS.

INTRODUCTION TO AMERICAN EDITION.

A BIOGRAPHY of the great Bering is of especial interest to American readers desiring an accurate history of a country that has recently come into our possession, and the adjoining regions where most of the geographical investigations of the intrepid Danish-Russian explorer were made. The thorough, concise, and patient work done by Mr. Lauridsen is deserving of world-wide commendation, while the translation into the language of our land by Professor Olson of the University of Wisconsin puts students of American historical geography under a debt for this labor of love rather than remuneration that cannot be easily paid, and which is not common in our country. It is a matter of no small national pride that the translation into the English language of a work so near American geographical interests should have been done by an American, rather than emanate from the Hakluyt Society or other British sources, from which we usually derive such valuable translations and compilations of old explorations and the doings of the first explorers.

The general American opinion regarding Bering is probably somewhat different from that on the continent which gave him birth and a patron government to carry out his gigantic and immortal plans; or, better speaking, it was different during the controversy in the past over the value and authenticity of the great explorer's works, for European opinion of Bering has slowly been more and more favorable to him, until it has reached the maximum and complete vindication in the admirable labors of Lauridsen, whose painstaking researches in the only archives where authentic data of the doings of the daring Dane could be found, has left no ground for those critics to stand upon, who have censured Peter the Great's selection of an oriental explorer. In short, America has always respected Bering as a great explorer, and oftentimes heralded him as one of the highest of heroes, whatever may have been the varying phases of European thought on the subject; and the reasons therefor, I think, are two-fold. In the first place, the continent which Bering first separated from the old world is yet a new country. Since its discovery, not only exploration, but commercial exploration, or pioneering as we call it, has been going on, and in this every one has taken his part or mingled often with those who have. Presidents who were pioneers, have been contemporaries with our times, while those who have struggled on the selvage of civilization are numerous among us, and their adventures as narrated in books are familiar stories to our ears. Such a people, I believe, are much less liable to listen to the labored logic of a critic against a man who carried his expedition six thousand miles across a wilderness and launched it on the inhospitable shores of an unknown sea, to solve a problem that has borne them fruit, than others not similarly situated would be. While the invariable rule has been that where the path-finder and critic—unless the critic has been an explorer in the same field— have come in collision, the latter has always gone to the wall, it is easy to see that with a jury that have themselves lived amidst similar, though possibly slighter, frontier fortunes, such a verdict is more readily reached.

The other reason, which is not so commendable, is that few Americans at large have interested themselves in the discussion, or in fact knew much about it. True, the criticisms on the Eastern continent have been re-echoed on this side of the water, and even added to, but they have created no general impression worth recording as such in a book that will undoubtedly have far wider circulation than the discussion has ever had, unless I have mis-judged the temper of the American people to desire information on just such work as Bering has done, and which for the first time is presented to them in anything like an authentic way by Professor Olson's translation of Mr. Lauridsen's work. I do not wish to be understood that we as a nation have been wholly

indifferent to Bering and the discussion of his claims. Far from it.
It has rather been that in invading the Bering world their disposition has led them to view the solid ground on which he made his
mark, rather than the clouds hovering above, and which this work
dissipates. It is rather of that character of ignorance—if so strong
a word is justifiable—that is found here in the persistent misspelling
of the great explorer's name and the bodies of water which have
transmitted it to posterity so well, although the authority—really
the absolute demand, if correctness is desired—for the change
from *Behring* to *Bering* has been well known to exist for a number
of years, and is now adopted in even our best elementary geogra-
phies. While the animalish axiom that "ignorance is bliss" is
probably never true, there may be cases where it is apparently
fortunate, and this may be so in that Americans in being seemingly apathetic have really escaped a discussion which after all has
ended in placing the man considered in about the same *status* that
they always assumed he had filled. One might argue that it would
have been better for Americans, therefore, if they had been presented with a simple and authentic biography of the immortal
Danish-Russian, rather than with a book that is both a biography
and a defense, but Lauridsen's work after all is the best, I think all
will agree, as no biography of Bering could be complete without
some account of that part in which he had no making and no
share, as well as that better part which he chronicled with his
own brain and brawn.

I doubt yet if Americans will take very much interest in the
dispute over Bering's simple claims in which he could take no
part; but that this book, which settles them so clearly, will be
welcomed by the reading classes of a nation that by acquisition in
Alaska has brought them so near the field of the labor of Bering,
I think there need not be the slightest fear. It is one of the most
important links yet welded by the wisdom of man which can be
made into a chain of history for our new acquisition whose history
is yet so imperfect, and will remain so, until Russian archives are
placed in the hands of those they consider fair-minded judges,
as in the present work.

On still broader grounds, it is to be hoped that this work will meet with American success, that it may be an entering wedge to that valuable literature of geographical research and exploration, which from incompatibility of language and other causes has never been fully or even comprehensively opened to English speaking people. It has been well said by one who has opportunities to fairly judge that "it has been known by scientists for some time that more valuable investigation was buried from sight in the Russian language than in any or all others. Few can imagine what activity in geographical, statistical, astronomical, and other research has gone on in the empire of the Czar. It is predicted that within ten years more students will take up the Russian language than those of other nations of Eastern Europe, simply as a necessity. This youngest family of the Aryans is moving westward with its ideas and literature, as well as its population and empire. There are no better explorers and no better recorders of investigations." It is undoubtedly a field in which Americans can reap a rich reward of geographical investigation. There is an idea among some, and even friends of Russia, that their travelers and explorers have not done themselves justice in recording their doings, but this in the broad sense is not true. Rather they have been poor chroniclers for the public; but their official reports, hidden away in government archives, are rich in their thorough investigations, oftentimes more nearly perfect and complete than the equivalents in our own language, where it takes no long argument to prove that great attention given to the public and popular account, has been at the expense of the similar qualities in the official report; while many expeditions, American and British, have not been under official patronage at all, which has seldom been the case with Russian research. As already noted, the bulk of similar volumes from other languages and other archives into the English has come from Great Britain; but probably from the unfortunate bitter antagonism between the two countries which has created an apathy in one and a suspicion in the other that they will not be judged in an unprejudiced way, Russia has not got a fair share of what she has really accomplished geographically translated into our tongue. It is through America, an unprejudiced nation, that this could be remedied, if a proper interest is shown, and which will probably be determined, in a greater or less degree, by the reception of this book here, although it comes to us in the round-about way of the Danish language.

FREDERICK SCHWATKA.

TRANSLATOR'S PREFACE.

IN placing before the American public this book on Vitus Bering, I desire to express my cordial thanks to those who by word and deed have assisted me. I am especially grateful to Lieutenant Frederick Schwatka, who, in the midst of pressing literary labors consequent on his recent explorations among the cave and cliff dwellers of the Sierra Madre Mountains, has been so exceedingly kind as to write an introduction to the American edition of this work. I feel confident that the introductory words of this doughty explorer will secure for Bering that consideration from the American people to which he is fairly entitled.

I find it a pleasant duty to acknowledge my indebtedness to Dr. Leonhard Stejneger of the Smithsonian Institution, who has sent me some valuable and interesting notes to the chapter on "The Stay on Bering Island" (Chapter XIX). Dr. Stejneger's notes are of especial interest, for in the years 1882–'84 he spent eighteen months on Bering Island in the service of the United States government, the object of his expedition being to study the general natural history of the island, to collect specimens of all kinds, but especially to search for remains of the sea-cow. He wished also to identify the places mentioned by Steller, the famous naturalist of the Bering expedition, in order to compare his description with the localities as they present themselves to-day, and to visit the places where Bering's vessel was wrecked, where the ill-fated expedition wintered, and where Steller made his observations on the sea-cow. The results of Dr. Stejneger's investigations have been published in "Proceedings of the United States National Museum" and in various American and European scientific journals.

I am also under obligation to Prof. Rasmus B. Anderson, Ex-United States Minister to Denmark, through whom I have been enabled to make this an authorized edition, and to Reuben G. Thwaites, Secretary of the Wisconsin State Historical Society, and Frederick J. Turner, Assistant Professor of American History in the University of Wisconsin, for valuable criticism and suggestions.

In regard to the orthography of Russian and Siberian names, I wish to say that I have endeavored to follow American writers that advocate a rational simplification. W. H. Dall, author of "Alaska and its Resources," says on this point: "From ignorance of the true phonetic value of the Russian compound consonants, and from literal transcription, instead of phonetic translation, of the German rendering of Russian and native names, much confusion has arisen. Many writers persistently represent the third letter of the Russian alphabet by *w*, writing Romanow instead of Romanoff, etc. The twenty-fifth letter is also frequently rendered *tsch* instead of *ch* soft, as in *church*, which fully represents it in English. It is as gross an error to spell *Kamchatka* for instance, *Kamtschatka*, as it would be for a foreigner to represent the English word *church* by *tschurtsch*, and so on." From this it would seem that the Germanized forms of these names are incorrect, as well as needlessly forbidding in appearance. It is, moreover, due to German writers that Bering's name has been burdened with a superfluous letter. Fac-similes of his autograph, one of which may be seen by referring to Map I. in the Appendix, prove incontestably that he spelled his name without an *h*.

Although Mr. Lauridsen's book is essentially a defense of Vitus Bering, written especially for the student of history and historical geography, it nevertheless contains several chapters of thrilling interest to the general reader. The closing chapters, for instance, give, not only a reliable account of the results of Bering's voyage of discovery in the North Pacific, and valuable scientific information concerning the remarkable animal life on Bering Island, where, before Bering's frail ship was dashed upon its shores, no human foot had trod, but they also portray in vivid colors the tragic events that brought this greatest of geographical enterprises to a close.

The regions to which Bering's last labors gave Russia the first title are at the present time the object of much newspaper comment. His last expedition, the few survivors of which brought home costly skins that evinced the great wealth of the newly discovered lands, opened up to the Russian fur-hunter an El Dorado that still continues to be a most profitable field of pursuit, now vigilantly watched by the jealous eyes of rival nations.

MADISON, WIS.   JULIUS E. OLSON.

AUTHOR'S PREFACE.

THROUGH the patronage of the Hielmstierne-Rosencrone Institution, obtained in the summer of 1883, I was enabled to spend some time among the archives and libraries in St. Petersburg, to prepare myself for undertaking this work on Vitus Bering. I very soon, however, encountered obstacles which unassisted I should not have been able to surmount; for, contrary to my expectations, all the original manuscripts and archives pertaining to the history of Bering were written in Russian, and the latter in such difficult language that none but native palæographers could read them.

I should for this reason have been compelled to return without having accomplished anything, had I not in two gentlemen, Admiral Th. Wessalgo and Mr. August Thornam of the telegraph department, found all the assistance that I needed. The Admiral is director of the department of hydrography, and has charge of the magnificent archives of the Admiralty. He is very familiar with the history of the Russian fleet, and he gave me, not only excellent and exhaustive bibliographical information, besides putting at my disposal the library of the department, but also had made for me copies of various things that were not easily accessible. He has, moreover, since my return been unwearied in furnishing me such information from the Russian archives as I have desired. For all of this kindness, enhanced by the Admiral's flattering remarks about Denmark and the Danes, I find it a pleasant duty to express my warmest thanks. To Mr. Thornam I am no less indebted. Notwithstanding his laborious duties in the central telegraph office of St. Petersburg, he found it possible week after week, often eight or ten hours out of the twenty-four, to assist me in translating the vast materials.

Besides this, I derived much benefit from his comprehensive knowledge of Siberia, obtained on travels in the same regions where Bering had been. He has had the kindness to examine the collection of charts and maps in both the Admiralty and Imperial libraries, and secure for me some valuable copies. He has also, at my request, examined a series of articles in periodicals containing notices of Bering's geographical enterprise.

It is only by means of this valuable assistance that I have succeeded in basing this biographical sketch on Russian literature, and putting it, as I hope, on a par with what has been written on this subject by Russian authors.

Of the many others that in one way or another have seconded my efforts in giving as valuable a biography of my renowned fellow-countryman as possible, I owe special thanks — not to mention the Hielmstierne-Rosencrone Institution — to Mr. Hegel, the veteran publisher, Col. Hoskier, Dr. Karl Verner, instructor in Sclavonic languages at the University of Copenhagen, who has examined some very difficult archival matter for me, Professor Alexander Vasilievich Grigorieff, Secretary of the Imperial Russian Geographical Society, and to Mr. E. W. Dahlgren, Secretary of the Swedish Society for Anthropology and Geography.   P. L.

PART I.

BERING'S FIRST EXPEDITION.

CHAPTER I.

RUSSIA AND ENGLAND IN THE WORK OF ARCTIC EXPLOR-
ATION.—VITUS BERING'S RANK AS AN EXPLORER.

IN the great work of Arctic exploration done during
the last two centuries, it was first Russia and later
England that took the lead, and to these two nations we
are principally indebted for our knowledge of Arctic con-
tinental coast-lines. The English expeditions were undertaken with better support, and under circumstances better
designed to attract public attention. They have, moreover, been excellently described, and are consequently well
known. But in the greatness of the tasks undertaken, in
the perseverance of their leaders, in difficulties, dangers,
and tragic fates, Russian explorations stand worthily at
their side. The geographical position of the Russians,
their dispersion throughout the coldest regions of the
earth, their frugal habits, remarkable power of foresight,
and their adventurous spirit, make them especially fitted
for Arctic explorations. Hence, as early as the first half
of the eighteenth century, they accomplished for Asia what
the English not until a hundred years later succeeded in
doing for the other side of the earth,—namely, the
charting of the polar coasts.

In this work the Russians introduced the system of
coasting and sledging into the service of Arctic expedi-

tions, and it is only through a systematic development of these means that western Europe has been enabled to celebrate its most brilliant triumphs in the Arctic regions, and to succeed in getting farther than did the navigators of the seventeenth century. The history of Russian polar explorations has a series of proud names, which lack only the pen of a Sherard Osborn to shine by the side of Franklin and McClure, and it redounds to the honor of Denmark that one of the first and greatest of these men was a Dane,—that the most brilliant chapter in the history of Russian explorations is due to the initiative and indefatigable energy of Vitus Bering. In the service of Peter the Great he successfully doubled the northeastern peninsula of Asia, and after his return he made a plan for the exploration of the whole Northeast passage from the White Sea to Japan. Although he succumbed in this undertaking, he lived ·long enough to see his gigantic plans approach realization.

Bering was buried on an island in the Pacific, amid the scenes of his labors, under that sand-barrow which had been his death-bed. For many generations only a plain wooden cross marked his resting-place, and as for his fame, it has been as humble and modest as his head-board. His labors belonged to a strange people who had but little sympathy for the man. His own countrymen, among whom he might have found this sympathetic interest, knew his work but very imperfectly. Not until after the lapse of a century did he find a careful biographer, and even within comparatively recent years the great scientist Von Baer has found it necessary to defend him against misunderstandings and petty attacks.

Danish literature contains nothing of moment concerning him, for the two treatises which several generations ago were published by M. Hallager and Odin Wolff, are merely scanty extracts from G. F. Müller's historical works. In the following pages, therefore, relying not only upon Russian, but also upon West European literature for information, we desire to erect to him a monument by giving a short account of his life and work, sketching at the same time a chapter of geographical history which is lacking neither in importance nor in interest.

CHAPTER II.

VITUS BERING was a son of Jonas Svendsen and his second wife, Anna Bering of Horsens, at which place he was born in the summer of 1681. On the maternal side he descended from the distinguished Bering family, which during the seventeenth and eighteenth centuries flourished in various parts of Denmark, and included a very respectable number of ministers and judicial officers.*

Our hero passed his childhood in a Christian family of culture in the Jutland seaport town of his birth. Here for a series of years his father filled several positions of trust, and was closely associated with the leading men of the place, as his wife's sister, Margaret Bering, had married two consecutive mayors. He was, however, far from being considered well-to-do. He had many children. One of his sons had caused him much trouble and expense, and was finally sent to the East Indies. In the probate record of his estate, made in 1719, there is a deed of conveyance from himself and wife in which the following

---

*Some details of Bering's genealogy, which can be of no interest to the American reader, the translator has taken the liberty to omit.

appears: "We are old, miserable, and decrepit people, in no way able to help ourselves. Our property consists of the old dilapidated home and the furniture thereto belonging, which is of but little value." It was his share of this inheritance, with accrued interest, all amounting to 140 *rigsdaler*, that Vitus Bering later presented to his native town to be used for the benefit of the poor.

From inclination, and forced by the circumstances of his humble home, Bering went to sea, and on the long expeditions that he made, he developed into an able seaman. From an East India expedition in 1703 he came to Amsterdam, where he made the acquaintance of Admiral Cruys, a native of Norway. Soon afterwards, at the age of twenty-two, he joined a Russian fleet as a sub-lieutenant. What Norwegian and Danish seamen accomplished at this period in the service of Russia, has been almost entirely forgotten. In the company of intelligent foreigners that Czar Peter employed for the transformation of his kingdom, the Danish-Norse contingent occupies a prominent place. This is due principally to Peter himself, and was a result of his experiences in Holland. After having, on his first extensive foreign trip, learned the art of ship-building,— not in Zaandam, as it is usually stated, but at the docks of the East India Company in Amsterdam,— he was much dissatisfied with the empirical method which the Hollanders. used, and he wrote to Voronetz, his own ship-yard, that the Dutch ship-builders there should no longer be permitted to work independently, but be placed under the supervision of Danes or Englishmen.

Peter retained his high regard for Danish-Norse ship-building during his whole life, and it was on this account that Danes and Norwegians were enabled to exert so great an influence in St. Petersburg. This is the reason, too, that Danish-Norse* seamen were received so kindly in Russia even long after the death of the great Czar.

Next to Peter, Norwegians and Danes had the greatest share in the founding of the Russian fleet, and among them the place of honor belongs to the Norseman Cornelius Cruys, who in 1697 was assistant master of ordnance in the Dutch navy, where he was held in high regard as a ship-builder, a cartographer, and as a man well versed in everything pertaining to the equipment of a fleet. Peter made him his vice-admiral, and assigned to him the technical control of the fleet, the building of new vessels, their equipment, and, above all, the task of supplying them with West European officers.

Weber assigns Cruys a place in the first rank among those foreigners to whom Russia owes much of her development, and remarks that it was he, "the incomparable master of ordnance, who put the Russian fleet upon its keel and upon the sea." He belonged to the fashionable circles of St. Petersburg, owned a large and beautiful palace on the Neva, where now tower the Winter Palace and the Hermitage, and was one of the few among the wealthy that enjoyed the privilege of entertaining the Czar on festive occasions. He became vice-president of the council of the Admiralty, was promoted, after the peace of Nystad, to the position of admiral of the Blue

* Norway and Denmark were at this time united.—TR.

Flag, and made a knight of the order of Alexander Nevsky.

In Peter the Great's remarkable house in St. Petersburg there is preserved, among many other relics, a yawl which is called the grandfather of the fleet. With this, Peter had begun his nautical experiments, and in 1723, when he celebrated the founding of his fleet, he rowed down the Neva in it. Peter himself was at the rudder, Apraxin was cockswain, and Admiral Cruys, Vice-Admiral Gordon, Sievers and Menshikoff were at the oars. On this occasion the Czar embraced Cruys and called him his father.

During his whole life Cruys preserved a warm affection for his native land; hence it was natural that the Scandinavian colony in St. Petersburg gathered about him. His successor as vice-president of the council of the Admiralty, and as master of ordnance, was the former Danish naval lieutenant Peter Sievers, who likewise elevated himself to most important positions, and exerted a highly beneficial influence upon the development of the Russian fleet. At the side of these two heroes, moreover, there were others, as Admirals Daniel Wilster and Peter Bredal, Commander Thure Trane, and also Skeving, Herzenberg, Peder Grib, "Tordenskjold's * brave comrade in arms," and many others.

For a long time Vitus Bering was one of Cruys's most intimate associates, and these two, with Admiral Sievers, form an honorable trio in that foreign navy. Bering was soon appointed to a position in the Baltic fleet, and

---

* Peter Tordenskjold (1691-1720), a Norwegian in the Danish Norse service,—the greatest naval hero Scandinavia has ever produced.—TR.

during Russia's protracted struggles, his energy found
that scope which he before had sought on the ocean, and
at the same time he had the satisfaction of fighting the
foes of his native land. He was a bold and able commander. During the whole war he cruised about in the
Sea of Azov and the Black Sea, and in the Baltic and
other northern waters. Some of the most important
transport expeditions were entrusted to him. The Czar
prized his services very highly, and when, after the misfortune at Pruth in 1711, he laid a plan to rescue three
of the best ships of his Black Sea fleet by a bold run
through the Bosporus, Vitus Bering, Peder Bredal, and
Simon Skop were chosen for the task. Whether the plan
was carried out, it is difficult to determine. Berch says
that it was not, and adds, "I cite the incident simply to
show that even at that time Bering was looked upon as
an excellent commander." In various West European
authorities, however, it is distinctly stated that Sievers
conducted the ships to England, and in a review of
Bering's life published by the Admiralty in 1882, it is
stated that Bering was in 1711 appointed to conduct the
ship Munker from the Sea of Azov to the Baltic, and as
the Admiralty would hardly in a condensed report have
taken notice of plans which had never been carried out,
it seems most probable that Berch has been incorrectly
informed.

In 1707 Bering was promoted to the position of lieutenant, in 1710 to that of lieutenant-captain, and in 1715
to that of captain of the fourth rank, when he assumed
command of the new ship Selafail in Archangel to sail it
to Copenhagen and Kronstadt. In 1716 he participated

in an expedition of the united fleets to Bornholm under the command of Sievers. In 1717 he was made captain of the third, and in 1720 of the second rank, and took part, until peace was concluded, in the various manœuvers in the Baltic under the command of Gordon and Apraxin.*

After the peace of Nystad in 1721, however, his position became somewhat unpleasant. Although he was a brother-in-law of Vice-Admiral Saunders, he had, according to Berch, powerful enemies in the Admiralty. The numerous promotions made after the conclusion of peace, in no way applied to him. In the following year younger comrades were advanced beyond him, and hence in 1724 he demanded promotion to a captaincy of the first rank, or his discharge. After protracted negotiations, and in spite of the fact that Apraxin repeatedly refused to sign his discharge, he finally obtained it, and then withdrew to his home in Viborg, Finland, where he owned an estate, and where, no doubt on account of the Scandinavian character of the city, he preferred to stay. During the negotiations for his discharge, the Czar was in Olonetz, but some time afterwards he informed Apraxin that Bering was again to enter the navy, and with the desired promotion. This occurred in August, 1724, and a few months later Bering was appointed chief of the *First Kamchatkan Expedition,* the object of which was to determine whether Asia and America were connected by land.

* See Appendix, Note 1.

CHAPTER III.

THE equipment of Bering's first expedition was one of
Peter the Great's last administrative acts. From his
death-bed his energy set in motion those forces which in
the generation succeeding him were to conquer a new
world for human knowledge. It was not until his mighty
spirit was about to depart this world that the work was
begun, but the impetus given by him was destined to be
effective for half a century; and the results achieved still
excite our admiration.

Peter was incited to undertake this work by a desire
for booty, by a keen, somewhat barbaric curiosity, and by
a just desire to know the natural boundaries of his
dominion. He was no doubt less influenced by the flat-
tery of the French Academy and other institutions than
is generally supposed. His great enterprise suddenly
brought Russia into the front rank of those nations which
at that time were doing geographical exploration. Just
before his death three great enterprises were planned:
the establishment of a mart at the mouth of the river
Kur for the oriental trade, the building up of a maritime trade with India, and an expedition to search for

the boundary between Asia and America. The first two projects did not survive the Czar, but Bering clung to the plan proposed for him, and accomplished his task.

Peter the Great gave no heed to obstacles, and never weighed the possibilities for the success of an enterprise. Consequently his plans were on a grand scale, but the means set aside for carrying them out were often entirely inadequate, and sometimes even wholly inapplicable. His instructions were usually imperious and laconic. To his commander-in-chief in Astrakhan he once wrote: "When fifteen boats arrive from Kazan, you will sail them to Baku and sack the town." His instructions to Bering are characteristic of his condensed and irregular style. They were written by himself, in December, 1724, five weeks before his death, and are substantially as follows : " I. At Kamchatka or somewhere else two decked boats are to be built. II. With these you are to sail northward along the coast, and as the end of the coast is not known this land is undoubtedly America. III. For this reason you are to inquire where the American coast begins, and go to some European colony; and when European ships are seen you are to ask what the coast is called, note it down, make a landing, obtain reliable information, and then, after having charted the coast, return."

After West Europe for two centuries had wearied itself with the question of a Northeast passage and made strenuous efforts to navigate the famed Strait of Anian, Russia undertook the task in a practical manner and went in search of the strait, before it started out on a voyage around the northern part of the old world.

Were Asia and America connected, or was there a strait between the two countries? Was there a North-west and a Northeast passage ? It was these great and interesting questions that were to be settled by Bering's first expedition. Peter himself had no faith in a strait. He had, however, no means of knowing anything about it, for at his death the east coast of Asia was known only as far as the island of Yezo. The Pacific coast of America had been explored and charted no farther than Cape Blanco, 43° north latitude, while all of the northern por-tion of the Pacific, its eastern and western coast-lines, its northern termination, and its relation to the polar sea, still awaited its discoverer.

The above-mentioned ukase shows that the Czar's inquisitive mind was dwelling on the possibility of being able, through northeastern Asia, to open a way to the rich European colonies in Central America. He knew neither the enormous extent of the far East nor the vastness of the ocean that separated it from the Spanish colonies. Yet even at that time, various representatives of the great empire living in northeastern Siberia had some knowledge of the relative situation of the two continents and could have given Bering's expedition valuable directions.

Rumors of the proximity of the American continent to the northeastern corner of Asia must very early have been transmitted through Siberia, for the geographers of the sixteenth century have the relative position of the two continents approximately correct. Thus on the Barents map of 1598, republished by J. J. Pontanus in 1611, a large continent towers above northeastern Asia with the superscription, "America Pars," the two countries being separated by the Strait of Anian * (Fretum Anian). On a map by Joducus Hondius, who died in 1611, East Siberia is drawn as a parallelogram projecting toward the northeast, and directly opposite and quite near the northeast corner of this figure a country is represented with the same superscription. This is found again in the map by Gerhard Mercator which accompanies Nicolai Witsen's "*Noord en Ost Tartarye*," 1705, and in several other sixteenth century atlases. It is quite impossible to determine how much of this apparent knowledge is due to vague reports combined with happy guessing, and how much to a practical desire for such a passage on the part of European navigators, whose expensive polar expeditions otherwise would be folly. This much is certain, however: Witsen and other leading geographers based their views on information received from Siberia and Russia.†

In the history of discoveries the spirit of human enterprise has fought its way through an incalculable number of mirages. These have aroused the imagination, caused agitations, debates, and discussions, but have usually veiled an earlier period's knowledge of the question. There are many re-discovered countries on our globe. So

---

* In Baron A. E. Nordenskjöld's review of the Danish edition of this work on Bering in the *Journal of the American Geographical Society*, Vol. XVII., p. 290, he says: "In Barents' map of 1598 there is not, as Mr. Lauridsen seems to suppose, anything original as to the delineation of the northern coast of Asia and the relative situation of Asia and America. In this respect Barents' map is only a reproduction of older maps, which, with regard to the delineation of the northern coast of Asia, are based upon pre-Columbian suppositions; and these again rest upon the story told by Pliny the Elder in the 'Historia Naturalis,' L. VII., 13, 17, about the northern limit of the world known to him," etc. The judicious reader can not fail to see that the renowned author here shoots far beyond the mark, for Pliny the Elder can hardly be supposed to have had any knowledge of "America Pars."—*Author's Note to American Edition.*

† Note 2.

in this case. The northwestern part of America wholly disappeared from the cartography of the seventeenth century, and through the influence of Witsen's and Homann's later maps it became customary to represent the eastern coast of Asia by a meridian passing a little east of Yakutsk, without any suggestions whatever in regard to its strongly marked peninsulas or to an adjacent western continent. But even these representations were originally Russian, and are undoubtedly due to the first original Russian atlas, published by Remesoff. They finally gave way to the geographical explorations of the eighteenth century, which began shortly after the accession of Peter the Great, having been provoked by political events and conditions.

By the treaty of Nertchinsk in 1689 the Yablonoi Mountains were established as the boundary line between Russia and China. By this means the way to the fertile lands of Amoor was barred to that indurate caste of Russian hussars and Cossacks who had conquered for the White Czar the vast tracts of Siberia. A second time they fell upon northeastern Siberia, pressing their way, as before, across uninhabited tundras along the northern ocean, and thence conquered the inhabited districts toward the south. They discovered the island of Liakhov, penetrated the country of the Chukchees, Koriaks, and Kamshadales, and at the Anadyr River, in Deshneff's old palisaded fort, they found that point of support from which they maintained Russia's power in the extreme northeast. In this way the Russians learned the enormous extent of the country; but as they had no exact locations, they formed a very incorrect opinion of its outlines, and estimated its length from west to east too small by forty degrees.

From the fort on the Anadyr, Kamchatka was conquered in the first years of the eighteenth century, and from here came the first information concerning America. In 1711 the Cossack Popoff visited the Chukchee peninsula, and here he heard that from either side of the peninsula, both from the "Kolymaic" Sea and the Gulf of Anadyr, an island could be seen in the distance, which the Chukchees called "the great land." This land they said they could reach in *baidars* (boats rowed by women) in one day. Here were found large forests of pine, cedar, and other trees, and also many different kinds of animals not found in their country. This reliable information concerning America seems at the time to have been known in other parts of Siberia only in the way of vague reports, and was soon confused with descriptions of islands in the Arctic.

Czar Peter, however, soon laid his adjusting hand upon these groping efforts. By the aid of Swedish prisoners of war, he opened the navigation from Okhotsk to Kamchatka, and thus avoided the circuitous route by way of the Anadyr. A Cossack by the name of Ivan Kosyrefski (the son of a Polish officer in Russian captivity) was ordered to explore the peninsula to its southern extremity, and also some of the Kurile Islands. In 1719 he officially despatched the surveyors Yevrinoff and Lushin to ascertain whether Asia and America were connected, but secretly he instructed them to go to the Kurile Islands to search for precious metals, especially a white mineral which the Japanese were said to obtain in

large quantities from the fifth or sixth island. Through
these various expeditions there was collected vast, although unscientific, materials for the more correct understanding of the geography of eastern Asia, the Sea of
Okhotsk, Kamchatka, the Kuriles, and Yezo. Even concerning the Island of Nipon (Hondo), shipwrecked Japanese had given valuable information. Simultaneously,
the northern coast about the mouth of the Kolyma, had
been explored by the Cossacks Viligin and Amossoff.
Through them the first information concerning the Bear
Islands and Wrangel Island found its way to Yakutsk.
The Cossack chief Shestakoff, who had traveled into the
northeastern regions toward the land of the Chukchees,
accepted the accounts of the former for his map, but as
he could neither read nor write, matters were most bewil-
deringly confused. Yet his representations were later
accepted by Strahlenberg and Joseph de l'Isle in their
maps.

CHAPTER IV.

BERING'S KNOWLEDGE OF SIBERIAN GEOGRAPHY.—TER-
RORS OF TRAVELING IN SIBERIA.—THE EXPEDITION
STARTS OUT.—THE JOURNEY FROM ST. PETERSBURG
TO THE PACIFIC.

AND now the question is, what did Bering know of
these efforts which had been made during the
decades preceding his expedition, and which in spite of
their unscientific character, were nevertheless of such
great importance in order to be able to initiate one's self
in the geography of eastern Asia? In the first place, the
surveyor Lushin, was a member of the Bering expedition,
and when Bering, in the summer of 1726, was sojourning
in Yakutsk, Shestakoff's nephew, who had accompanied
his uncle on his expedition against the Chukchees, became an attaché of Bering's expedition, while the elder
Shestakoff had gone to Russia to collect means for the
contemplated military expedition. Furthermore, Ivan
Kosyrefski, who in the meantime had become a monk,
was also staying in Yakutsk, and his valuable report preserved in the voivode's (governor's) office was now sur-
rendered to Bering. Thus we see that Bering was in
personal contact with the men, who, in the decade preceding, were the chief possessors of geographical knowledge concerning those northeastern regions.

In the second place, he received in Yakutsk information concerning Deshneff's journey in 1648 from the Kolyma to the Anadyr River. Although this journey was first critically discussed by G. F. Müller,* its main features were nevertheless well known in Siberia, and are referred to, among other places, in Strahlenberg's book, whence the results appear in Bellini's map in Peter Charlesvoix's "*Histoire du Japan*," published in 1735. Unfortunately, however, Bering seems to have had no knowledge of Popoff's expedition to the Chukchees peninsula and his information concerning the adjacent American continent, or of Strahlenberg's outline maps, which were not published until after his departure from St. Petersburg.

Bering's two expeditions are unique in the history of Arctic explorations. His real starting point was on the extremest outskirts of the earth, where only the hunter and yassak-collector had preceded him. Kamchatka was at that time just as wild a region as Boothia or the coasts of Smith's Sound are in our day, and, practically viewed, it was far more distant from St. Petersburg than any known point now is from us. One hundred and thirty degrees—several thousand miles—the earth's most inhospitable tracts, the coldest regions on the globe, mountains, endless steppes, impenetrable forests, morasses, and fields of trackless snow were still between him and the mouth of the Kamchatka River, and thither he was to lead, not a small expedition, but an enormous provision train and large quantities of material for ship-building. On the journey,

* Note 3.

river-boats had to be built by the score, and also two ships. Now his course was up the swift streams of Siberia, and now on horseback or in sledges drawn by dogs through the dreary and desolate forests of the Yakuts and Tunguses. He employed several hundred laborers and twice as many horses to do work which modern ships can accomplish in a few weeks. Franklin, Mackenzie, Schwatka, and many others have traversed vast tracts of the Arctic regions, but their expeditions in light sledges can not be compared with those burdensome transports which Bering and his men dragged from the Gulf of Finland to the shores of the Pacific.

In the early part of the year 1725 the expedition was ready to start out from St. Petersburg. The officers were the two Danes, Vitus Bering, captain and chief, and Martin Spangberg, lieutenant and second in command, and also the following: Lieut. Alexei Chirikoff, Second Lieut. Peter Chaplin, the cartographers Luskin and Patiloff, the mates, Richard Engel and George Morison, Dr. Niemann, and Rev. Ilarion.* The subordinates were principally sailors, carpenters, sailmakers, blacksmiths, and other mechanics.

Peter the Great died Jan. 28, 1725; † but a part of the expedition under the command of Lieut. Chirikoff had already started on the 24th; Bering followed Feb. 5. They passed the whole of the first summer in toilsome expeditions overland and on rivers in western Siberia. March 16, they arrived at Tobolsk, whence, in May, the journey was continued with four rafts and seven boats by way of the rivers Irtish, Obi,

* Note 4.   † Here as elsewhere, Old Style.

Ket, Yenisei, Tunguska, and Ilim, through regions
where there was scarcely a Russian *isba,* on rivers which
were dangerous on account of hidden rocks and skerries,
and where progress was constantly interrupted by the
transporting that had to be done between the streams.
September 29, the expedition arrived at the town of
Ilimsk and had to pass the winter there. Meanwhile,
however, Lieut. Chaplin had, in the spring, been sent
in advance to Yakutsk, in order, at the voivode's (governor's) to hasten the preparations for transportation in
the direction of Okhotsk, whither he was to send a
small command who were to fell trees and begin the
work of shipbuilding. Bering * himself went to Irkutsk
to obtain from the governor there information concerning the climate and physical features of Eastern Siberia,
the modes of travel, and means of transportation in
that distant and little known country. Spangberg was
sent with mechanics and soldiers to the Kut, a tributary of the Lena, for the purpose of cutting timber and
building vessels for the voyages to be made in the spring.
At Ustkutsk there were built in all fifteen barges
(about 45 feet long, 12 feet wide and 15 inches deep) and
fourteen boats. On May 8, 1726, Spangberg sailed for
Yakutsk, and somewhat later Chirikoff started off with
the rear. By the middle of June, the expedition was
gathered at the capital of East Siberia, which at that
time had three hundred houses. Here Bering remained
until the 16th of August, busily engaged in making
preparations for the difficult journey eastward. He
had made two thousand leathern sacks for transporting

* Note 5.

flour to Okhotsk, and gave the voivode orders to keep in readiness six hundred horses to forward other necessaries for the expedition.

From this point the expedition traveled an entirely untrodden path, and the 1026 versts (685 miles) to Okhotsk were a severe test of its endurance. Even in our day, this journey can be made only under the greatest difficulties. The region is rough and mountainous, and intersected by deep streams without bridges or other means of crossing. The traveler must traverse dangerous swamps and tundras, or cut his way through dense forests. In the winter the difficulties are doubled. Horses, reindeer, and dogs soon become exhausted on these unbroken roads. A space cleared in the snow, where the cooking, eating, and sleeping are done, is the only shelter. The temperature falls to — 46° R. (71° Fahrenheit). Clothing must be changed daily to avoid dampness, and when the *poorgas* (blizzards) sweep over the snowy wastes, a few steps from camp are often fatal. This is a description of that region in our day, and it was hardly any more inviting over a hundred and fifty years ago.

It was found necessary to divide the expedition. The branching tributaries of the Lena offered possibilities for transportation which had to be taken advantage of. Hence, as early as July 7, Lieut. Spangberg was sent by river with thirteen rafts loaded with materials, and a force of 204 workmen to reach Yudomskaya Krest by way of the tributaries Aldan, Maya, and Yudoma, and thence across a ridge down to the river Urak, which flows into the Sea of Okhotsk. The overland expeditions, consisting of 800 horses, were sent in various directions. Bering himself started out on August 16, with 200 horses, and after a journey of forty-five days, reached Okhotsk. The journey was a very difficult one. The horses sought in vain for food under the deep snow. Scores of them were overcome by hunger and exhaustion. The severe cold caused the forces much suffering and hardship, nor did they find but few comforts when they reached Okhotsk in the latter part of October. The town consisted of only eleven huts, with ten Russian families, who supported themselves by fishing. Here, too, many of the horses died for lack of food, and a herd of heifers sent there by Shestakoff was lost from the same cause. Only one survived the winter. It was now necessary to build huts for the winter. The whole of November was spent in felling trees, and not until December 2, could Bering take shelter under a roof of his own. On the other hand, the ship for the expedition was on the stocks, and in spite of all troubles and privations, Bering found time to push forward vigorously its construction.

Spangberg, however, fared worst of all. Winter took him by surprise two hundred and seventy-five miles from Yudomskaya Krest, the nearest inhabited place, in an entirely barren and swampy region where he could not obtain the slightest assistance. His boats and the bulk of their provisions had to be left at the confluence of the Yorbovaya and the Yudoma, while he and his men, with what provisions they could take with them on the hand-sleds, started out for Okhotsk on foot.

Meanwhile, the severity of the winter increased, the mercury congealed, and the snow was soon six feet deep. This forced them to leave their sleds, and for eight full weeks after November 4, these travelers sought shelter every night in the snows of Siberia, wrapped in all the furs they could possibly get hold of. Their provisions were soon exhausted, famine soon became a companion to cold, and matters even came to such a pass that they were compelled to try to maintain life by gnawing "straps, leathern bags, and shoes." They would surely have starved to death, had they not accidentally happened to strike Bering's route, where they found dead horses and a few hundred-weights of flour. December 21, Bering received from Spangberg a message, relating that he had started for Yudomskaya Krest with ninety-six sledges, and that he had left the boats in charge of a mate and six guards. Bering immediately dispatched ten sledges with provisions for his relief, and on the succeeding day, thirty-seven sledges with thirty-nine men. January 6, 1727, Spangberg reached Okhotsk, and a few days later his whole command had arrived, eighteen of whom were now sick. Twice during the course of the winter, Spangberg and Chaplin were obliged to repeat this journey to rescue the materials at the Yudoma. Not until midsummer, 1727, did the rear under the command of Chirikoff arrive from Yakutsk.

And yet Bering was far from the place where his work of discovery could begin. On June 8, the new ship Fortuna was launched and equipped for the prospective voyage. Moreover, the ship that had been

used in exploring the Sea of Okhotsk in 1716 arrived,
and after thorough repairs was put into the service.

Bering's next objective point was the mouth of the
river Bolshoya in southwestern Kamchatka. From the
mouth of this river, which is navigable for small vessels, he took the Cossack route to the interior, first up
the Bolshoya to the tributary Byistraya, then up this
to within forty versts of its source, thence across a port-
age to the Kamchatka, the mouth of which was his
real objective point. From this position he would be
able to fall back upon the Russian colony, which com-
prised a number of unimportant stockaded forts on
the Bolshoya and Kamchatka rivers, and could
also gain support from that control of the natives
which was exercised from this point. This change of
base could have been much more easily and quickly
accomplished by sailing around the Kamchatka Peninsula, but this was something that had never been done.
No accurate information was to be had in regard to the
waters, or to the location of any place. Possibly Bering
had not as yet been able to disabuse his mind of the
prevalent delusions concerning the great extent of Kamchatka. In the second place, he was no doubt unwilling
to trust his invaluable stores in the inferior vessels
built at Okhotsk. Hence he took the old route.

July 1, Spangberg sailed with the Fortuna for
Bolsheretsk, accompanied by thirteen Siberian traders.
Two days láter Chirikoff brought up the rear from
Yakutsk. Somewhat later, the quartermaster arrived
with 110 horses and 200 sacks of flour. A week later
63 horses more arrived, on July 20, one soldier with

80 horses, and by the 30th over 150 horses more, and also 50 oxen.

August 11, Spangberg returned from his voyage to the Bolshoya River, and on the 19th the whole command went on board,—some on the Fortuna and others on the old vessel. Their destination was the Bolshoya, situated 650 miles from Okhotsk, where they arrived September 4. Here the cargoes were transferred to boats and, in the course of the month of September, brought to the fort, a simple log fortress with seventeen Russian dwellings and a chapel, twenty miles from the sea. It took the whole winter to traverse, first with boats and later with sledges, the 585 miles across Kamchatka, from Bolsheretsk to the lower Kamchatka fort. Under the greatest difficulties, the expedition now followed the course of the Kamchatka River, camping at night in the snow, and enduring many a fierce struggle with the inclement weather. The natives were summoned from far and near to assist in transporting their goods, but the undertaking proved fatal to many of them. Finally on March 11, 1728, Bering reached his destination, the lower Kamchatka Ostrog,* where he found forty huts scattered along the banks of the river, a fort, and a church. A handful of Cossacks lived here. They occupied huts built above the surface of the ground. They did not always eat their fish raw, but in other respects lived like the natives, and were in no regard much more civilized than they. The fort was located twenty miles from the sea, surrounded by forests of larch, which yielded excellent

* An Ostrog is a stockaded post or village.

material for ship-building. From this point the exploring party proper was to start out.*

* Note 6.

CHAPTER V.

BERING now found himself upon the bleak shores of
an Arctic sea, with no other resources than those he
had brought with him, or could extort from these barren
tracts. He again began the work of ship-building, and
in the summer of 1728, a ship called the Gabriel, staunch
enough to weather a heavy sea, was launched. The
timber for this vessel had been hauled to the ship-yard by
dogs; the tar they had prepared themselves, while rigging, cable, and anchors had been dragged nearly two
thousand miles through one of the most desolate regions
of the earth. And as for the provisions, they would certainly strike terror in the hearts of Arctic explorers of
to-day. "Fish oil was his butter, and dried fish his beef
and pork. Salt he was obliged to get from the sea," and
according to the directions of the Cossacks he distilled
spirits from "sweet straw."* Thus supplied with a
year's provisions, he started upon his voyage of discovery
along an unknown coast and on an unknown sea. "It is
certain," says Dr. Campbell concerning Bering at this
stage, "that no person better fitted for this undertaking
could have been found; no difficulty, no danger daunted

*Note 7
29

him. With untiring industry and almost incredible patience he overcame those difficulties which to anyone else would have seemed insurmountable."

On July 9, the Gabriel started down the river, and on the 13th the sails were hoisted. The crew numbered forty-four men: namely, one captain, two lieutenants, one second lieutenant, one physician, one quartermaster, eight sailors, one saddler, one rope-maker, five carpenters, one bailiff, two Cossacks, nine soldiers, six servants, one drummer, and two interpreters. Bering's point of departure was the lower Kamchatka fort, situated 160° 50' east of Greenwich, the variation of the compass being 13° 10' E. The latitude of the cape at the mouth of the Kamchatka River was determined as 56° 3' N., which agrees with the observations made by Cook, who was very near this point on his last voyage. The day was reckoned from 12 o'clock at noon, on which account his dating does not correspond with that of civil time; hence, the 16th of August with him began on the 15th, at noon. The mile of the journal is the Italian mile, which is somewhat longer than the English mile. Bering's course was nearly all the time along the coast, in from nine to twelve fathoms of water, and usually with land in sight to the north and west. On July 27, they passed Cape St. Thaddeus at a distance of three miles, and here the sea seemed fairly alive with spotted whales, seals, sea-lions, and dolphins. After having sailed past the Anadyr River, without quite being able to find their bearings in regions of which they had not a single astronomical determination, and where they were not successful in finding any natives, they finally, on July 31, saw land extending along the northern horizon, and soon afterwards sailed into the Bay of the Holy Cross (St. Kresta Bay) where the Gabriel spent two days under sail in search of fresh water and a place to anchor. On the 2d of August the latitude was determined as 60° 50′ N., whereupon the voyage was continued to the southeast along the high and rocky coast, where every indentation was very carefully explored. August 6, the Gabriel lay in the Bay of Preobrashensky, and on the 7th, Chaplin was sent ashore to obtain water from a mountain stream. On his way he found huts, where there had quite recently been Chukchees, and in various places he found foot-paths, but met no human beings. On the 8th, Bering sailed along the coast in a south southeasterly direction. At 7 o'clock, a boat containing eight men was seen rowing toward the vessel. They did not, however, dare to approach the Gabriel, but at last one of the number jumped into the water, and on two inflated seal bladders swam out to the ship, and announced, by the aid of the two Koriak interpreters, that they were Chukchees, and that their people lived along the coast, that they knew the Russians well, that the Anadyr River lay far to the west, that the continent extended in the same direction, and that they would soon get sight of an island. The Koriaks, however, understood his language only imperfectly, and the journal regrets that they were on this account prevented from obtaining further important information. Bering gave him some small presents and sent him back to try to persuade his companions to come on board. They approached the vessel, but suddenly turned and disappeared. The longitude was 64° 41′.

August 9, Cape Chukotskoi was doubled, an important event in the history of this expedition,—an event which Müller, in order to make results fit into his frame, has not even mentioned. The name, it is true, is not found in the journal, but it appears on Bering's chart in Du Halde's work, which Müller knew. Bering determined the southern extremity of the cape to be 64° 18', Cook 64° 13'.

August 11, the weather was calm and cloudy. At 2 o'clock in the afternoon, they saw an island toward the southeast, which Bering, in honor of the day, called St. Lawrence. At noon the latitude was found to be 64° 20', and hence the Gabriel was in the strait between Asia and America.

August 12, there was a light breeze and cloudy weather. On this day they sailed sixty-nine miles, but the difference in latitude was only 29'. At sunset the longitude was computed by the aid of the variation of the needle to be 25° 31' east of the lower Kamchatka fort, or 187° 21' east of Greenwich.

August 13, a fresh breeze and cloudy. Bering sailed during the whole day with land in sight, and the difference in latitude was only 78'.

August 14, weather calm and cloudy. They sailed 29 miles + 8¾ miles for the current. The course of the current was from south southeast to north northwest. At noon the latitude was 66° 41' when they saw high land astern, and three hours later high mountains. (East Cape is 66° 6' N. lat. and 190° 21' east of Greenwich.)

August 15, gentle wind, cloudy weather. From noon until 3 o'clock Bering sailed to the northeast, and after having sailed seven miles in this direction, he determined to turn back. At 3 o'clock he announced, that as he had now accomplished his task, it was his duty, according to his orders, to return. His bearings were then 67° 18' N. latitude, and 30° 19' east of the Kamchatka fort, or 193° 7' east of Greenwich. In Du Halde, where Bering himself gives his reasons, it is stated : "This was Captain Bering's most northerly point. He thought that he had accomplished his task and obeyed orders, especially as he no longer could see the coast extending toward the north in the same way. *(Surtout, parcequ'il ne voyait plus que les terres continuassent de courier de même du côté du Nord.")* Moreover, if they should go farther, he feared, in case they should have adverse winds that they might not be able to return to Kamchatka before the end of the summer, and how were they to be able to pass the winter in such a climate, liable to fall into the hands of a people who had not yet been subjugated, and who were human only in outward appearance.*

When Bering turned about, his command was to steer south by west, half west. In this course they sailed with the wind at a rate of more than seven miles an hour. At 9 o'clock in the morning, they saw a high mountain on the right, where Chukchees lived, and to the left and seaward they saw an island, which in honor of the day they called Diomede.† This day they sailed 115 miles, and reached latitude 66° 2'.

On August 17, Bering again passed the narrowest part of the strait. The weather was cloudy, there was a fresh breeze, and they sailed along the Asiatic coast, where

they saw many Chukchees, and at two places they saw
dwellings. The natives fled at the sight of the ship. At
3 o'clock very high land and mountains were passed.
With a very good breeze, they had been enabled to sail
164 miles, and an observation showed that they were in
latitude 64° 27'. According to this, Bering was out of
the strait and getting farther and farther away from the
American continent.

August 18, the wind was light and the weather clear.
On the 20th, beyond the Island of St. Lawrence, he met
other Chukchees, who told him that they had made journeys from the Kolyma River westward to Olenek, but
that they never went by sea. They knew of the Anadyr
fort which lay farther to the south; on this coast there
dwelt people of their race; others they did not know.

After a storm on the 31st of August, in which the
main and foresail were rent, the anchor cable was broken
and the anchor lost, they reached the mouth of the Kamchatka at 5 o'clock P. M., September 2, 1728.

CHAPTER VI.

BERING turned back because he felt convinced that
he had sailed around the northeastern corner of
Asia, and had demonstrated that in this part of the
earth the two great continents were not connected.
The third point in his orders was of course dropped,
for along the Siberian coasts of the Arctic sea, he could
expect to find neither European colonists nor ships;
hence, further search with this object in view would be
vain. He had a very clear idea of the general outline
of eastern Asia, and this knowledge was based upon the
facts of his own voyage, the information he had obtained in Yakutsk about Deshneff's expedition from
Kolyma to Anadyr, and upon the account which the
natives gave of the country and of their commercial
journeys westward to Olenek.

He was, moreover, convinced that he had given the
search for a Northeast passage a rational foundation,
and his thoughts on this subject are found clearly presented in a correspondence from St. Petersburg to a
Copenhagen periodical, *Nye Tidende*, in 1730, whence
the following: "*Bering has ascertained that there really*

does exist a Northeast passage, and that from the Lena River it is possible, provided one is not prevented by polar ice, to sail to Kamchatka, and thence to Japan, China, and the East Indies." This correspondence, which appeared immediately after his return on the first of March, 1730, originated either with him or with some of his immediate friends, and shows that he fully appreciated the extent of his discovery.* It was this conviction that led him to undertake his next great enterprise, the navigating and charting of the Northeast passage from the Obi River to Japan,—from the known West to the known East.

Unfortunately, however, the principal result of his work remains as above stated. An unhappy fate prevented him from discovering the adjacent American continent. At the narrowest place, Bering Strait is 39 miles wide; and hence, under favorable conditions, it is possible to see simultaneously the coast-lines of both continents.† Cook, more fortunate than Bering, was enabled to do this, for when he approached the strait, the sun dispersed the fog, and at one glance both continents were seen. With Bering it was otherwise, for, as we have seen from his journal, the weather during the whole time that he was in the strait, · both on the voyage up and back, was dark and cloudy. Not until the 18th of August did the weather clear up, but as the Gabriel was sailing before a sharp breeze, he was then too far away to see land on the other side. "This," Von Baer exclaims, "must be called *bad luck.*"

* Note 10.   † Note 11.

We may possibly feel inclined to blame Bering for his haste. Why did he not cruise about in the region of 65° to 67° north latitude ? A few hours' sailing would have brought him to the American coast. This objection may, however, prove to be illegitimate. The geographical explorer, as well as every other investigator, has a right to be judged from the standpoint of his times, and on the basis of his own premises. Bering had no apprehension of an adjacent continent, partly on account of the Koriak interpreter's imperfect knowledge of the Chukchee tongue, partly as a result of the fact that the knowledge of the times concerning the western coast of America was very meager. This knowledge extended no farther than to 43° north latitude,—to Cape Blanco in California; hence, in the nature of things, he could not be expected to search for land which presumably he knew nothing of. But here we must also take into consideration his poor equipment. His cables, ropes, and sails were in such bad condition, after the three years' transport through Siberia, that he could not weather a storm, and his stock of provisions was running so low that it put an unpleasant check on any inclination to overreach his main object, and this, as we have seen, did not include the exploration of an American coast, if separated from Asia. To explore a new coast thirteen degrees of latitude and thirty degrees of longitude in extent, and make such a chart of it that its outline is comparatively correct, and which, for a long time, was far superior to anything made afterward,* ought certainly to be considered

* Note 12.

a splendid result, when we remember that the objects of
the expedition were entirely of a nautico-geographical
character. Bering's determinations of longitude in East
Siberia were the first made there, and through them it
was ascertained that the country extended thirty degrees farther toward the east than was supposed. His
observations were based on two eclipses of the moon in
Kamchatka in the years 1728 and 1729,* and although
they were not entirely accurate, they vary so little, that
the general position of the country was established.
And hence we are not surprised to find that no one has
given Bering a better testimonial than his great and
more fortunate successor, Captain Cook. He says: † "In
justice to the memory of Bering, I must say, that he has
delineated the coast very well, and fixed the latitude and
longitude of the points better than could be expected
from the methods he had to go by." Yes, Captain Cook
found it necessary to defend Bering against the only
official report of the expedition which at that time had
appeared, and more than once he puts in proper relief
Bering's sober investigations, as compared with Müller's
fancies and guesses. Before the time of Cook, it had
been customary to depreciate Bering's work; ‡ but since
that time Admiral Lütke, a hundred years after Bering's
death, has defended his reputation, and Berch, who very
carefully perused his journals, repeatedly expresses his
admiration for the accuracy with which the nautical
computations were made. This statement is made after
a comparison of results with those obtained by Captain
Cook.

* Note 13.   † Note 14.   ‡ Note 15.

Furthermore, as has already been said, Bering was not aware of the fact that he was sailing in a comparatively narrow sound,—in that strait which has carried his name to posterity. He saw nothing beyond the nearest of the Diomede Islands, that is to say, the middle of the strait ; and this island, as we have seen, is mentioned in the journal and on the chart, with the latitude correctly given.* His name was not immediately associated with these regions. The first place, so far as I am able to ascertain, that the name Bering Strait appears, is on a map which accompanies Rob. de Vangondie's "*Memoire sur les pays de l'Asie,*" Paris, 1774. But it is especially to Captain Cook's high-mindedness that the name was retained, for it was used in his great work. Later, Reinholdt Forster, who characterizes Bering as "a meritorious and truly great navigator," triumphantly fought his cause against Büsching and others.†

But even at the present time, an interesting misunderstanding attaches to this part of Bering's history and the cartography of these regions. In our Arctic literature and on all our polar maps, it is asserted that Vitus Bering, on his first voyage, turned back at Cape Serdze Kamen. That such a supposition has been able to maintain itself, only shows how little the original sources of his history are known in West Europe, and how unheeded they have been in Russia. About a hundred years ago the Danish Admiral De Löwenörn and the English hydrographer A. Dalrymple showed that Frobisher Strait had by some ignorant hand been located on the east coast of Greenland,

* Note 16.   † Note 17.

while it was in reality located on the coast of *Meta incognita* beyond Davis Strait.* A similar error presents itself in connection with Serdze Kamen. It can be historically established that this name has been the object of a double change, and that the present Serdze Kamen on the northern coast of the Chukchee peninsula, has nothing whatever to do with the history of Bering and his voyage. This misunderstanding is, however, not of recent date, for as early as in the first decade after the voyage, it was assumed that Bering's course, even after he had passed East Cape, was along the coast. Thus I find on a map by Hazius in Nuremberg, 1738,† and other maps of about the same time, based on Bering's map as given by Du Halde, that the Gabriel's turning point is marked by a star near the coast with the same latitude as the present Serdze Kamen, with the following explanation : *" Terminus litorum a Navarcho Beerings recognitorum."* This supposition gradually gained ground in West Europe as well as in Russia, especially so, too, as Bering's new expedition and consequent death°prevented him from correcting the error, and as there for a generation was nothing more known of the voyage than the resumé which appears in Du Halde's work. Moreover, the manner in which the coast-line in Bering's original map is extended beyond East Cape, has only served to strengthen the opinion. The fact is that Serdze Kamen was a name unknown to Bering. It is found neither on his map, in his own account, nor in the ship's journal, and could not be so found for a very obvious reason— Bering had never been there.

After having passed East Cape on the 14th of August, he no longer sailed along the coast. On that day at noon they still saw land astern, and three hours later, high mountains, but during the succeeding forty-eight hours land was seen neither to the east nor the west.

As we have seen, the journal gives the turning point as 4° 44' east of Cape Chukotskoi, and Dr. Campbell gives another series of astronomical determinations, sent by Bering from Kamchatka to the Senate in St. Petersburg, and these show in a striking way that the turning point was east of the northeastern corner of Asia.

According to these :*

The Island of St. Lawrence is 64° north latitude and 122° 55' east of Tobolsk.

The Island of Diomede is 66° north latitude and 125° 42' east of Tobolsk.

The turning point, 67° 18' north latitude and 126° 7' east of Tobolsk.

Hence, Serdze Kamen (67° 3' north latitude and 188° 11' east of Greenwich), as Bercht† expressly remarks, must have lain more than four degrees west of the turning point. That this must have been so appears also from the course of the vessel on its return, west southwest, which would have been impossible, if the Gabriel had been near the north coast, intending to return through the strait. Among recent writers, Von Baer‡ alone critically calls attention to these facts, without, however, thoroughly investigating the case. This I shall now attempt to do.

* Note 20.   † Note 21.   ‡ Note 22.

The name Serdze Kamen appears for the first time—historically speaking—in Gerhard Fr. Müller's *Sammlung Russischer Geschichte*, Vol. III., 1758.* He says: "Bering finally, in a latitude of 67° 18', reached a headland whence the coast recedes to the west. From this the captain drew the very plausible conclusion that he now had reached the most northeasterly point of Asia. But here we are forced to admit that the circumstance upon which the captain based his conclusion was false, as it has since been learned that the above-mentioned headland was identical with the one called Serdze Kamen by the inhabitants of Fort Anadyr, on account of the promontory being heart-shaped." Even this looks suspicious. The account of some ignorant Cossacks is presented as a corrective to the report of educated navigators, and it is also indicated that the garrison at Fort Anadyr had exact knowledge of the northern coast of the Chukchee peninsula, something it did not have at all.†

But in order to understand Müller, it is necessary to make a slight digression. When Bering, in the summer of 1729, was on his return to St. Petersburg, he met, between Okhotsk and Yakutsk, the Cossack chief Shestakoff, who by the aid of Bering's ships intended to undertake an extensive military expedition in the eastern seas. He soon fell, however, in an engagement, but his comrade Captain Pavlutski led an invasion into the land of the Chukchees. From Fort Anadyr he went northward to the Arctic Ocean, thence along the coast toward the east, then across the Chukchee peninsula to the Pacific. A more detailed account than this cannot be given, for his

route as indicated on Müller's map is an impossible one.
This much, however, seems to be irrefutable: shortly
after having crossed the Chukchee peninsula in a southerly direction, he came to a sea, and this sea could be no
other than Bering Sea.* Moreover, it appears from the
account, that he was on his return to the fort. Müller
goes on to say : "From here he sent a part of his men in
boats, whither he himself with the majority of the party
proceeded by land, following the shore, which at this
place extended toward the southeast. Those in boats
were so near the shore that they reported to him every
evening. On the seventh day, the party in boats came to
the mouth of a river, and twelve days later, to the mouth
of another. At about seven miles from this point there
extends eastward far into the sea a headland, which is
first mountainous, but then flat, as far as the eye can
reach. This headland is probably what induced Captain
Bering to turn back. Among the mountains on this promontory there is one which, as already noted, is by the
natives of Anadyrskoi Ostrog called Serdze Kamen.
From here Pavlutski started for the interior." On this
loose reasoning rests Serdze Kamen,—a process of reasoning which attempts to show clearly that this headland
must be a point on the Pacific coast, and that it must
have lain many days' journey west of Bering Strait.
But how is it possible, that Müller could have been so
confused as to make such strange blunders? The case
could not thus have presented itself to him. On the
basis of Deshneff's journey and Pavlutski's cruise, he
formed in his imagination a picture of northeastern

* Note 25.

Siberia, in which the Chukchee peninsula assumed a double horned shape, or—as Von Baer expresses it—resembled a bull's horn.

He used Bering's chart as a foundation when he had no other, but he omitted Cape Chukotskoi, and on the 66th parallel he inserted Serdze Kamen. From this point he made the coast recede, first westward, then northward and eastward to a large circular peninsula situated between 72°–75° north latitude, which he called Chukotskoi Noss. It is this imaginary peninsula which Pavlutski crosses. He accordingly reaches the Pacific coast to the north of Bering Strait, and in this way Müller succeeds in locating Serdze Kamen north of the strait. Hence, according to Müller's opinion, Bering had never doubled the northeastern corner of Asia, and he had never been out of the Pacific. "And although the coast beyond Serdze Kamen," he says, "turns westward, it forms only a large bay, and the coast-line again takes a northerly direction to Chukotskoi Noss, a large peninsula in a latitude of 70° or more, and where it would first be possible to say authoritatively that the two hemispheres were not connected. But how could all this have been known on the ship? The correct idea of the shape of the land of the Chukchees and the peninsula bearing the same name, is due to geographical investigations instituted by me at Yakutsk in 1736 and 1737."

Blinded by the archival dust of Yakutsk, Müller confused everything. Cape Chukotskoi, which Bering had found to be in latitude 64° 18' N., was placed beyond 72° N.; Bering's most northerly point, which lay far out in the sea, was changed to a headland in latitude 66° N.,

and, misled by some vague reports from the garrison at
Fort Anadyr, he called this point Serdze Kamen. Everything is guess-work!

But where did Müller get his Serdze Kamen, and
what place was it that the garrison at Fort Anadyr called
by this name? For of the extreme northeast part of the
peninsula, or the details of Bering's voyage — especially
as early as in 1730 — they could have had no knowledge.
The explanation is not difficult. On Russian maps of the
last century, those of Pallas and Billings, for example,*
there is found on the eastern shore of St. Kresta Bay, somewhat northeast of the mouth of the Anadyr, a cape which
bears the name of Serdze Kamen. As Bering does not have
this name, and as it seems to have been known as early as at
the time of Pavlutski, it must have originated either with
him and the Cossacks at the fort, or with the Chukchees.
Sauer relates the following concerning the origin of the
name: "Serdze Kamen is a very remarkable mountain
projecting into the bay at Anadyr. The land side of this
mountain has many caves, to which the Chukchees fled
when Pavlutski attacked them, and from where they
killed a large number of Russians as they passed. Pavlutski was consequently obliged to seek reinforcements at
Anadyr, where he told that the Chukchees shot his men
from the *heart* of the *cliff*, and hence it received the
name of Serdze Kamen, or the heart-cliff." But this
account, which finds no authority whatever in Sauer's
work, is severely criticised by Lütke, who calls attention
to the fact that the Chukchees called a mountain on the
eastern shore of the St. Kresta Bay *Linglin Gaï*, that is,

*Note 26.

the heart-cliff. It is quite improbable that they got this
name from the Cossacks in Anadyrsk, and hence we here
undoubtedly have the origin of the name.*

In Steller's various works one can see what confused
ideas concerning Bering's first expedition the academists
who wrote his history really had. They succeeded in
bringing confusion into the simplest questions, and, as a
result, wrecked his reputation. In Steller's description of
Kamchatka, where he enumerates the headlands of the
peninsula, a remarkable statement is found, which offers
excellent proof of the correctness of Lütke's opinion.†
The situation of Serdze Kamen between East Cape and
the mouth of the Anadyr is here distinctly given.
Hence, according to his opinion, Bering reached no
farther than to St. Kresta Bay, and the sarcastic remarks
plainly show Steller's partisan view.‡ Müller was not so
rash. When he moved Cape Chukotskoi half a dozen
degrees farther to the north, he moved Serdze Kamen
also, and *carried it from St. Kresta Bay up into Bering
Strait.*

In this cool move he was fortunate enough to get into
a closer agreement with Bering's determination of latitude, but unfortunately hit upon new difficulties. His
own map is based upon Bering's, as he had no other, but
Bering's voyage did not, as is well known, end at any
headland. Neither his chart nor his journal supports

---

* Note 27.

† The passage is: "*Das Tschuktschische Vorgebürge in Nord Osten*, (elsewhere he locates it in latitude 66° N.), *ein anderes 2 Grad ohngefaehr süd-
licher, Sirza-kamen, der Herzstein gennent, der auch bey der ersten Expedition
der herzlichen Courage der See-Officier die Gränzen gesetzt. Ohnweit demselben
ist eine sehr groze Einbucht und guter Hafen, auch vor die grösesten Fahrzenge;
Das Anadirskische Vorgebürge. . . . .*"

‡ Note 28.

any such theory, and hence Müller, either accidentally or purposely, does not in his book have a word about the voyage from the 10th to the 15th of August, and on his map (1758) Bering's "track" is broken off near East Cape. This headland is Müller's Serdze Kamen,* a fact of which even a very cursory glance at Müller's and Bering's maps will convince any one. But even Bering had located the northeastern corner of Asia (East Cape) a few minutes too far northward, and in order to make the map coincide with his theory and with Bering's computations, Müller made the error greater, without, however, fixing it at Bering's turning-point, but at 67° 18' N. lat., where, according to Bering's and his own account, it ought to be.

Thus matters stood up to the time of Cook's third voyage. But as Cook had on board, not only Müller's book and map in an English translation, but also Bering's map, and an excellent treatise by Dr. Campbell in Harris's Collection of Voyages, he could pass judgment while at the place in question. As a matter of course he upholds Bering. Hence, it was a natural result that Serdze Kamen, which, as we have seen, was to coincide with the most northerly point reached by Bering, could no longer retain its position in the latitude of East Cape, which was more than a degree too far south; and in order to make Müller's account intelligible, Captain Cook had the choice between entirely expunging the name, or bringing it up to an approximately correct latitude. Cook chose the latter; and to this mistake on his part it is due that the last splinter of Müller's vain structure

* Note 29.

passed into the cartography of the future. In latitude
67° 3′ N., Cook found a projecting promontory with
many crags and peaks, and "possibly one or another of
them may be heart-shaped. This peak we have, on Müller's authority, called Serdze Kamen." *

Here then we have the third Serdze Kamen, and we
can now see how it has wandered about the northeast
corner of Asia. As a matter of fact, it is situated in a
latitude nearly the same as the most northerly point
reached by Bering, but unfortunately this does not at all
answer Müller's description. It does not project eastward into the sea, but on the contrary, its main direction
is toward the northwest. At the base of this headland,
the coast does not in a striking manner extend toward
the west, but continues in its former direction. Nor does
it consist of steep rocks and a low point extending farther than the eye can reach. In other words, the present
Serdze Kamen has nothing whatever to do either with
Bering's voyage or Müller's description.†

To this period of Bering's history another observation
must be made. In his excellent treatise entitled, "What
Geography owes to Peter the Great," Von Baer tries to
show that Bering turned back in his course, not on the
15th, but on the 16th of August, and that too, notwithstanding the fact that both Bering and Müller, in print,
give the former date,—yes, notwithstanding the fact that
Von Baer himself had an autograph card from Bering
which likewise gives the 15th. In his criticism on this
point, Von Baer based his statements on those extracts of
the ship's journal referred to above, which as we have

* Note 30.   † Note 31 and Map I. in Appendix.

seen give the 16th of August, and this, in his opinion, must be decisive. But the disagreement in these sources is only an apparent one. As we already have noted, Bering reckoned the day from 12 o'clock at noon. Hence the journal's 16th of August began at noon on the 15th of August, and as Bering turned back at 3 o'clock in the afternoon, this occurred on the 15th of August according to the calendar, and on the 16th of August according to the artificial day of the journal. Thus Von Baer's correction is based on a misunderstanding.* That this view of the question is correct is seen also from that passage in the journal where the Island of St. Lawrence is mentioned. According to the journal this island was passed at 2 o'clock P. M. on the 11th of August, and Berch, to whom we are indebted for information concerning Bering's day, is, strange to say, surprised to think that Bering named the island in honor of the saint of the preceding day, notwithstanding that the 11th at 2 o'clock P. M. is in reality, according to the calendar day, the 10th of August, St. Lawrence Day. The first twelve hours of the journal's day belong to the preceding day. Hence, Bering turned back August 15, at 3 o'clock P. M.

*Note 32.

CHAPTER VII.

BERING'S WINTER AT THE FORT.—INDICATIONS OF AN
ADJACENT CONTINENT.—UNSUCCESSFUL SEARCH FOR
THIS CONTINENT.—RETURN TO ST. PETERSBURG.—
GENERAL REVIEW OF THE RESULTS OF THE FIRST
EXPEDITION.

WHEN Bering on the 2d of September, 1728,
entered the mouth of the river Kamchatka, he
met the Fortuna, which had made a voyage around the
Kamchatka Peninsula. Who commanded the vessel on
this voyage, can not be ascertained.

Bering wintered at the fort. On the days that it was
light, the men were busy at work or receiving instructions, and thus the winter passed without any remarkable occurrences or misfortunes. Spangberg, however, was
obliged, on account of illness, to go to Bolsheretsk.*

At lower Kamchatskoi Ostrog, Bering became convinced that there must be a large wooded country not
far to the east. The waves were more like those of a
sea than of an ocean. The driftwood did not indicate
the flora of eastern Asia, and the depth of the sea grew
less toward the north; the east wind brought drift-
ice to the mouth of the river after three days, the
north wind, on the other hand, after five days. The

---

* A port on the southern coast of Kamchatka.

birds of passage came to Kamchatka from the east. The reports of the natives corroborated his inferences. They declared that they were able, in very clear weather, to see land in the east (Bering Island), and that in the year 1715 a man had stranded there, who said that his native land was far to the east and had large rivers and forests with very high trees. All this led Bering to believe that a large country lay toward the northeast at no very great distance.

In the summer of 1729, he started out to find this country, leaving the mouth of the Kamchatka for the east, July 6. If the wind had been favorable, he would very soon have reached Bering Island, where twelve years later he was buried. He must have been very near this island, invisible to him, however, on account of a fog; but on the 8th of July he was struck by a severe storm, which the frail vessel and the weather-worn rigging could not defy, and hence on the 9th, he headed for the southern point of Kamchatka. But also on this voyage he did geographical service by determining the location of the peninsula and the northern Kurile Islands, as well as exploring the channel between them, and thus finding for the Russian mariner a new and easier route to Kamchatka. Berch says, that although Bering had adverse winds on the voyage to Bolsheretsk, all his computations are quite accurate; the difference in latitude between the latter place and lower Kamchatka Ostrog is given as 6° 29', which is very nearly correct. Bering likewise determined the location of Cape Lopatka at 51° N. lat.

At Bolsheretsk Bering collected his men, distributed
provisions and powder, left the Fortuna with a crew
of one corporal and eleven men, and on the 14th of
July steered for Okhotsk. After a fortunate, but not
otherwise remarkable, journey, he reached St. Petersburg on the 1st of March, 1730. "From the perusal
of his ship's journal," says Berch, "one becomes convinced that our famous Bering was an extraordinarily
able and skillful officer ; and if we consider his defect-
ive instruments, his great hardships, and the obstacles
that had to be overcome, his observations and the great
accuracy of his journal deserve the highest praise. He
was a man who did Russia honor."

Bering had thus done good work in the service of
Asiatic geography. He had shown that he possessed
an explorer's most important qualification—never to
make positive statements where there is no definite
knowledge. By virtue of his extensive travels in northeastern Asia, his scientific qualifications, his ability to
make careful, accurate observations, and his own astronomical determinations, and by virtue of his direct
acquaintance with Kosyrefsky's and Lushin's works, he
was in a position to form a more correct opinion than
any contemporary concerning this part of the earth.
In spite of these great advantages in his favor, his
work was rejected by the leading authorities in St.
Petersburg. It is true that Bering found sincere support in the able and influential Ivan Kirilovich Kiriloff,
but to no one else could he turn for a just and competent judge. The great Russian empire had not yet
produced a scientific aristocracy. The Academy of

Science, which had been founded five or six years previous, was not composed of able scholars, but of a number of more or less talented contestants for honor and
fame,—of men who occupied a prominent yet disputed
position in a foreign and hostile country—young, hot-
headed Germans and Frenchmen who had not yet
achieved complete literary recognition. Such people
are stern and severe judges. Bering was unfortunate
enough to fall into the hands of the German Gerhard
Fr. Müller and the Frenchman Joseph Nicolas De l'Isle.

Although Müller had not yet seen Siberia, and
although it was not until ten years later that he succeeded in building that geographical card-house which
Captain Cook so noiselessly blew down, he nevertheless,
even at that time, on every occasion expressed the opinion that Bering had not reached the northeast point
of Asia, and that his voyage had consequently not
accomplished its purpose. De l'Isle was Bering's intel-
lectual antipode. As a geographer he delighted in
moving about on the borderland of the world's unex-
plored regions. His element was that of vaguest con-
jecture,— the boldest combinations of known and
unknown ; and even as an old man he did not shrink
from the task of constructing, from insufficient accounts
of travels and apocryphal sailor-stories, a map of the
Pacific, of which not a single line has been retained. He
overstrained himself on the fame of his deceased brother,
whose methods, inclinations, and valuable geographical
collections he had inherited, but unfortunately not that
intuitive insight which made Guillaume De l'Isle the

leading geographer of his age.   Hence, as a geographer,
he was merely an echo of his brother.

One of Guillaume De l'Isle's most famous essays had
been on the island of Yezo.   In 1643 the stadtholder of
Batavia, the able Van Diemen, sent the ships Kastri-
kon and Breskens under the command of Martin de
Vries and Hendrick Corneliszoon Schaep to Japan for
the purpose of navigating the east coast of the island of
Nipon (Hondo), and thence go in search of America by
sailing in a northwesterly direction to the 45th degree of
latitude; but in case they did not find America, which
people continued to believe lay in these regions, they
were to turn toward the northeast and seek the coast of
Asia on the 56th degree of latitude.   De Vries partly
carried out his chimerical project.   At 40° north latitude
he saw the coast of Nipon, two degrees farther north,
the snow-capped mountains of Yezo, and thence sailed
between the two Kuriles lying farthest to the south,
which he called Staaten Eiland and Kompagniland.   He
then continued his voyage into the Sea of Okhotsk to
48° north latitude, where he turned about, saw Yezo in
latitude 45°, but came, without noticing La Perouse
Strait, over to Saghalin, which he considered a part of
Yezo, and as he followed the coast of Saghalin to Cape
Patience in latitude 48°, he thought Yezo a very extensive island on the eastern coast of Asia.   Through the
cartography of the seventeenth century, for example
Witsen's and Homann's Atlas, but especially through Guillaume De l'Isle's globes and maps, these erroneous ideas
were scattered over the earth, and, when the first accounts
of Kamchatka, without being accompanied by a single

astronomical determination, reached Europe, many believed that this land was identical with Yezo. But as
De Vries had left some determinations of latitude and
longitude which showed that the island must be very near
Japan, some went even so far as to suppose that it was
contiguous to Nipon; indeed, Guillaume De l'Isle's essay
attempted to prove this. Thus three lands were made
one, while De Vries's Staaten Eiland and Kompagniland,
which could find no place in this series, were forced eastward into the Pacific as large tracts of land separated
from Kamchatka-Yezo and from each other by narrow
straits. But this is not all. The Portuguese cosmo-
grapher Texeïra had in 1649, in these same regions, indicated a coast projecting far to the east toward America,
seen by Juan de Gama on a voyage to New Spain from
the Philippine Islands. This Gamaland was now described as a continuation of Kompagniland. In Homann's
Atlas, 1709, it is represented as a part of America, and
Guillaume De l'Isle varied on the theme in a different
way.*

Unfortunately these ideas held sway in the scientific
world when Bering, in 1730, returned. Furthermore,
scholars thought these ideas were confirmed by Swedish
prisoners of war who had returned from Siberia, especially by the famous Tabbert, or Strahlenberg, as he was
later called, whose various imaginary chart-outlines had
been adopted in Homann's Atlas, 1727, and in other West
European geographical works then in vogue.†

Bering returned. His sober accounts and accurate
maps, in which there was nothing imaginary whatever,

* See Maps II. and III.   † Note 33.

were now to take up the fight against these prejudices.
Bering declared that he had sailed around Kamchatka
without having seen anything of these lands, although he
had—in a different direction, however—noticed signs of
land. On his map, Kamchatka was represented as a definitely defined region, and hence Guillaume De l'Isle's
structure had received its first blow, in case Bering's
representations should be accepted. But Bering's reputation had been undermined in still another direction.
The above-mentioned Cossack chief Shestakoff had, during his sojourn in Russia, distributed various rough contour sketches of northeastern Asia. This brave warrior,
however, knew just as little about wielding a pen as he
did a pencil. The matter of a few degrees more or less in
some coast-lines did not seriously trouble him. Even his
own drawings did not agree. Northeast of the Chukchee
peninsula he had sketched an extensive country, which
Bering had not seen.

It is characteristic of Joseph De l'Isle that he accepted
both Shestakoff and Strahlenberg, and as late as in 1753
still clung to their outlines. In the first place, it satisfied
his family pride to be able to maintain his brother's views
of the cartography of these regions (and of his views
Strahlenberg's were but an echo), and it moreover satisfied his predisposition to that which was vague and hypo-
thetical. At first De l'Isle succeeded in carrying out his
wishes, and in 1737 the Academy published a map of Asia
in which it would prove extremely difficult to find any
trace of Bering's discoveries.* It was accordingly quite
the proper thing to consider Bering's first expedition

* Note 34.

wholly, or at least to a great extent, unsuccessful. In
the literature of that day there are evidences of this,
especially in Steller's writings. He treats Bering with
scornful superiority, which is particularly out of place,
as he shows himself a poor judge in geographical matters.* Kiriloff, who in his general map of Russia in
1734† unreservedly accepted Bering's map, was the only
man who gave him due recognition. The Academy could
not persuade itself to make use of the only scientifically
obtained outline map in existence of the remotest regions
of the empire, until Bering, many years afterwards, had
won full recognition in Paris, Nuremberg, and London.
Bering's map was made in Moscow in 1731, and the Russian government presented it to the king of Poland,‡
who gave it to the Jesuit father Du Halde. He had it
printed and inserted in D'Anville's *Nouvelle Atlas de la
Chine*, a supplement to his large work on China, to which
we have several times referred.§ Of this work Dr. Campbell later gave an account in Harris's Collection of Voyages, and it was, furthermore, the basis of the better
class of geographical works on eastern Asia of last century until Captain Cook's day. A copy of the eastern
half of the map will be found in the appendix to this
treatise.

* Note 35.   † Note 36.   ‡ Note 37.   § Note 38.

PART II.

THE GREAT NORTHERN EXPEDITION.

CHAPTER VIII.

ARCTIC exploration has a bewitching power over its devotees. Bering and his companions did not escape the enchantment. Hardly had they returned from a five years' sojourn in the extremest corner of the world, when they declared themselves willing to start out again. As they had met with so much doubt and opposition from scholars,—had learned that the world's youngest marine lacked the courage to recognize its own contributions to science, and, furthermore, as the Admiralty thought it had given strong reasons for doubting Bering's results,* he proposed to make his future explorations on a larger scale and remove all doubt, by charting the whole of this disputed part of the globe.

April 30, 1730, only two months after his return, he presented two plans to the Admiralty. These have been found and published by Berch, and are of the greatest importance in judging of Bering's true relation to the Great Northern Expedition. In the first of these propositions he sets forth a series of suggestions for the administration of East Siberia, and for a better utiliza-

* Note 39.

tion of its resources. He desired, among other things, missionary work among the Yakuts, better discipline among the East Siberian Cossacks, more honesty among the yassak-collectors, the opening of iron mines at Okhotsk and Udinsk, and various other things. But it was never his intention to carry out these propositions himself, and it was a great mistake for the government to burden his instructions with such purely administrative work.

His second proposition is incomparably more interesting. In this he indicates the general outline of his Great Northern Expedition, the greatest geographical enterprise that the world has hitherto known. This document shows that he was the originator of the plan, something that has been contradicted, and but for this document might still stand contradicted. He proposed to start out from Kamchatka to explore and chart the western coast of America and establish commercial relations with that country, thence to visit Japan and Amoor for the same purpose, and finally to chart either by land or sea the Arctic coast of Siberia,—namely, from the Obi to the Lena.* Through these three enterprises and his former expedition, it was Bering's object to fill the vacant space on his chart between the known West and the known East,—between the Kara Sea and the Japan Islands. He refused to corroborate his first observations by again visiting the same localities, and he rightly concluded, that absolute proof of the separation of the continents would be ascertained if the American coast were charted.

* Note 40.

The political situation in the empire favored the adoption of Bering's plans. The Duchess of Courland, Anna Ivanovna, had just (1730) ascended the throne. With her the foreigners and Peter's reform party again came into power, and with much more zeal than skill, they sought to continue Peter's work. Anna aimed to shine in Europe as the ruler of a great power, and in Russia as a West European queen. Europe was to be awed by Russian greatness, and Russia by European wisdom. In one of his high-flown speeches Czar Peter had given assurance that science would forsake its abodes in West Europe, and in the fullness of time cast a halo of immortal glory around the name of Russia.

It was necessary to speed this time. Anna and her coadjutors had an insatiable desire for the splendor and exterior luster of culture. Like upstarts in wealth they sought to surround themselves with some of that glory which only gray-haired honor can bestow. One of the surest ways to this glory was through the equipment of scientific expeditions. They had at their disposal an academy of science, a fleet, and the resources of a mighty empire. The sacrifice of a few thousand human lives troubled them but little, and they exerted themselves to make the enterprise as large and sensational as possible. Bering's above-mentioned proposition was taken as a foundation for these plans, but when, after the lapse of two years, his proposition left the various departments of the government — the Senate, the Academy, and the Admiralty — it had assumed such proportions that he found great difficulty in recognizing it.

After having on April 30, 1730, submitted to the
Admiralty his new proposition, together with the accounts and reports of his first expedition, Bering was sent
to Moscow, where Anna maintained her court during the
first few years of her reign. Here he laid his plans
before the Senate, and made the map before referred to;
but all the leading men were then too much occupied
with court intrigues to be able to give his plans any of
their attention. Separated from his family, he wearied
of life in Moscow, and on January 5, 1732, the Senate
gave him leave of absence to go to St. Petersburg, on
condition that Chaplin and the steward would conclude
the reports. Moreover, the Senate ordered that the
Admiralty should pay Bering's claims against the government for his services. In view of the hardships he had
endured, he received 1,000 rubles, double the amount to
which he was entitled according to the regulations of the
department. Almost simultaneously he was promoted, in
regular succession, to the position of *capitain-command-
eur* in the Russian fleet, the next position below that of
rear-admiral.

In the spring of 1732, Anna, Biron, and Ostermann
had succeeded in crushing the Old Russian opposition.
The leaders of this party, especially the family of Dolgoruki, had been either banished to Siberia or scattered
about in the provinces and in fortresses, and now there
was nothing to hinder the government in pursuing its
plans. As early as April 17, the Empress* ordered that

---

*H. H. Bancroft, Vol. XXXIII., p. 42, History of Alaska, San Francisco,
1886, is in error when he states that this empress was Elizabeth, the daughter
of Peter the Great. Anna Ivanovna, a daughter of Peter the Great's half-
brother Ivan, was at this time on the throne. She reigned from 1730 to 1740.
Elizabeth Petrovna did not become empress until 1741.—Tr.

Bering's proposition should be executed, and charged the Senate to take the necessary steps for this purpose. The Senate, presided over by Ivan Kiriloff, an enthusiastic admirer of Peter the Great, acted with dispatch. On May 2, it promulgated two ukases, in which it declared the objects of the expedition, and sought to indicate the necessary means. Although the Senate here in the main followed Bering's own proposition and made a triple expedition (an American, a Japanese, and an Arctic), it nevertheless betrayed a peculiar inclination to burden the chief of the expedition with tasks most remote from his own original plans. It directed him not only to explore the Shantar Islands and reach the Spanish possessions in America, something that Bering had never thought of, but also included in its ukase a series of recommendations for the development of Siberia,—recommendations which Bering had previously made to the government, and which had already provoked some definite efforts, as the exiled Pissarjeff, a former officer of the Senate, had been removed to Okhotsk to develop that region and extend the maritime relations on the Pacific.

He seems, however, not to have accomplished anything, and the Senate thought it feasible to burden Bering with a part of this task. He was directed to supply Okhotsk with more inhabitants, to introduce cattle-raising on the Pacific coast, to found schools in Okhotsk for both elementary and nautical instruction, to establish a dock-yard in this out-of-the-way corner, to transport men and horses to Yudomskaya Krest, and to establish iron-works at Yakutsk, Udinsk, and other places. But this was simply the beginning of the avalanche, and

as it rolled along down through the Admiralty and
Academy, it assumed most startling dimensions. These
authorities aspired to nothing less than raising all human
knowledge one step higher. The Admiralty desired the
expedition to undertake the nautical charting of the Old
World from Archangel to Nipon — even to Mexico; and
the Academy could not be satisfied with anything less
than a scientific exploration of all northern Asia. As a
beginning, Joseph Nicolas De l' Isle, professor of astronomy at the Academy, was instructed to give a graphic
account of the present state of knowledge of the North
Pacific, and in a memoir to give Bering instructions how
to find America from the East. The Senate also decreed
that the former's brother, Louis, surnamed La Croyère,
an adventurer of somewhat questionable character, should
accompany the expedition as astronomer. Thus decree
after decree followed in rapid succession. On December
28, the Senate issued a lengthy ukase, which, in sixteen
paragraphs, outlined *in extenso* the nautico-geographical
explorations to be undertaken by the expedition. Com-
modore Bering and Lieut. Chirikoff, guided by the instructions of the Academy, were to sail to America with
two ships for the purpose of charting the American coast.
They were to be accompanied by La Croyère, who, with
the assistance of the surveyors Krassilnikoff and Popoff,
was to undertake a series of local observations through
Siberia, along several of the largest rivers of the country
and in its more important regions, across the Pacific, and
also along the coast of the New World. With three ships
Spangberg was to sail to the Kurile Islands, Japan, and
the still more southerly parts of Asia, while simultan-

eously the coast from Okhotsk to Uda, to Tugur, to the
mouth of the Amoor, and the coasts of the Shantar
Islands and Saghalin were to be charted.

Even these tasks exceeded all reasonable demands, and
not until several generations later did Cook, La Perouse,
and Vancouver succeed in accomplishing what the Russian Senate in a few pen-strokes directed Bering to do.
And yet, not until the government touched the Arctic
side of this task, did it entirely lose sight of all reason.
Its instructions to Bering were, not only to chart the
coast of the Old World from the Dwina to the Pacific, to
explore harbors and estuaries along this coast, to describe
the country and study its natural resources, especially its
mineral wealth, but also to dispatch an expedition to the
Bear Islands, off the mouth of the Kolyma, and to see to
it that his earlier trip to the Chukchee peninsula was
repeated, besides sailing from there to America, as the
results of his former voyage "were unsatisfactory," reliable information concerning that country having been
received from the Cossack Melnikoff.

All these expeditions were to start out from the great
Siberian rivers,—from the Dwina to the Obi with two
vessels under the charge of the Admiralty ; from the Obi
and Lena with three twenty-four-oared boats, two of
which were to meet between these two rivers, and the
third was to sail around Bering's Peninsula (thus Reclus
calls the Chukchee peninsula), or, if America proved to
be connected with that country, it was to attempt to find
European colonies. The orders of the Senate were, furthermore, to the effect that surveyors should be sent out
in advance for the preliminary charting of these river-

mouths, and to erect light-houses, establish magazines for convenient relays, and procure provisions and other necessaries,—very excellent directions, all of which, however, were so many meaningless words after they had left the government departments. Our age, which still has in mind the Franklin expeditions—the English parallel— is able to form an idea of these gigantic demands, and yet the Senate did not hesitate to load the organization of all this upon the shoulders of one man. Bering was made chief of all the enterprises east of the Ural Mountains. At the Obi and the Lena, at Okhotsk and Kamchatka, he was to furnish ships, provisions, and transportation.

But in spite of all that was vague and visionary in these plans, they had nevertheless a certain homogeneity. They were all nautical expeditions for nautical purposes and nautico-geographical investigations. Then the Academy added its demands, making everything doubly complicated. It demanded a scientific exploration of all Siberia and Kamchatka,—not only an account of these regions based on astronomical determinations and geodetic surveys, on minute descriptions and artistically executed landscape pictures, on barometric, thermometric, and aerometric observations, as well as investigations in all the branches of natural history, but it demanded also a detailed presentation of the ethnography, colonization, and history of the country, together with a multitude of special investigations in widely different directions. The leading spirits in these enterprises were two young and zealous Germans, the chemist Johann Georg Gmelin and the historian Gerhard Friedrich Müller, twenty-eight and twenty-four years of age respectively, members of the Academy, and later, highly respected scholars. Müller was a personal friend of Bering, and through him got a desire to participate in the expedition.

Kiriloff, the secretary of the Senate, himself a successful student of geography, supported the efforts of the Academy, and most generously gratified all the exaggerated demands that only imperious and inexperienced devotees of science could present. Indeed, Bering could not but finally consider himself fortunate in escaping a sub-expedition to Central Asia, one of Kiriloff's pet plans, which the latter afterwards took upon himself to carry out. The Academic branch of the expedition, which thus came to consist of the astronomer La Croyère, the physicist Gmelin (the elder), and the historian Müller, was right luxuriously equipped. It was accompanied by two landscape painters, one surgeon, one interpreter, one instrument-maker, five surveyors, six scientific assistants, and fourteen body-guards. Moreover, this convoy grew like an avalanche, as it worked its way into Siberia. La Croyère had nine wagon-loads of instruments, among them telescopes thirteen and fifteen feet in length. These Academical gentlemen had at least thirty-six horses, and on the large rivers, they could demand boats with cabins. They carried with them a library of several hundred volumes, not only of scientific and historical works in their specialties, but also of the Latin classics and such light reading as Robinson Crusoe and Gulliver's Travels. Besides, they had seventy reams of writing paper and an enormous supply of artists' colors, draughting materials and apparatus. All archives were to be open to them, all Siberian government authorities were to be at their service and furnish interpreters, guides, and laborers. The Professors, as they were called, constituted an itinerant academy. They drafted their own instructions, and no superior authority took upon itself to make these subservient to the interests of the expedition as a whole. From February, 1734, they held one or two weekly meetings and passed independent resolutions. It became a part of Bering's task to move this cumbersome machine, this learned republic, from St. Petersburg to Kamchatka, to care for their comforts and conveniences, and render possible the flank movements and side sallies that either scientific demands or their own freaks of will might dictate. In the original instructions such directions were by no means few. But Bering had no authority over these men. They were willing to recognize his authority only when they needed his assistance. None of them except Bering and his former associates had any idea of the mode and conditions of travel in that barbarous country. That there should be lack of understanding between men with such different objects in view as academists and naval officers, is not very strange. Their only bond of union was the Senate's senseless ukase. If it had been the purpose of the government to exhibit a human parallel to the "happy families" of menageries, it could hardly have acted differently. In all his movements Bering was hampered by this academical dead-weight. The Professors not only showed a lack of appreciation of Bering's efforts in their behalf, but they also stormed him with complaints, filled their records with them, and concluded them—characteristically enough—

with a resolution to prefer formal charges against him before the Senate.

Only a new state, as the Russian then was, only a government that recently had seen the will of one energetic man turn topsy-turvy a whole people's mode of life, and yet had preserved a fanciful faith in Peter the Great's teachings—his supreme disregard for obstacles,—only such a government could even think of heaping such mountains of enterprises one upon the other, or demand that any one man, and a foreigner at that, should carry them into execution.   Peter's spirit undoubtedly hovered over these plans, but the marble sarcophagus in the church of St. Peter and St. Paul had long since received his earthly remains, and without his personal energy the Senate's plans were but the projects of a dazzled fancy. On paper the Senate might indeed refer Bering to various ways and means ; it might enjoin upon the Siberian authorities to do everything in their power to promote the progress of the various expeditions ; it might direct its secretaries to prepare very humane declamation denouncing the practice of any violence against, or oppression of, the weak nomadic tribes in the East ; but it could not by a few pen-strokes increase the natural resources of Siberia, or change the unwillingness of the local authorities to accede to the inordinate demands which the nautical expedition necessarily had to make, nor could it make roads in the wild forest-regions where only the Yakut and Tunguse roamed about.   The Senate's humanitarian phrases were of but little significance to the explorers when it was found necessary to compel the nomads of the East to supply what the government

had failed to furnish. The Senate had ventured so near
the extreme limits of the possible, that it could not but
end by crossing the border and demanding the impossible.
These numerous expeditions, scattered over half a continent, were exposed to so many unforeseeable accidents
and misfortunes, that the government, in order to render
support and retain its control, would necessarily have to
be in regular communication. But east of Moscow there
was no mail service. Hence the government instructed
Bering to establish, on consultation with the local authorities, postal communication, partly monthly and partly
bi-monthly, from Moscow to Kamchatka, to the Chinese
border by way of Irkutsk, and by a new route to Uda,—
as though such a matter could be accomplished through
consultation. The Senate might have known, and in
fact did know, that in the mountainous forest-region
between Yakutsk and Okhotsk (a distance of about seven
hundred miles) there was but one single Russian hut,
and that all the requisites for a mail service — men,
horses, and roads — demanded unlimited means and most
extensive preparations.

A number of plans and propositions of minor importance are here omitted. The object has been to show, in
a succinct review, the origin of the Great Northern Expedition, its enormous compass, and the grouping of its
various enterprises about Vitus Bering as its chief. Von
Baer classes the tasks to be accomplished by Bering, each
of which demanded separately equipped expeditions,
under seven heads: namely, astronomical observations
and determinations in Siberia, physico-geographical explorations, historic-ethnographical studies, the charting

of the Arctic coast, the navigation of the East Siberian coast, and the discovery of Japan and America. This writer adds that no other geographical enterprise, not even the charting of China by the Jesuits, Mackenzie's travels, or Franklin's expeditions, can in greatness or sacrifice be compared with the gigantic undertakings that were loaded upon Bering, and carried out by him.*

It would no doubt be wrong to ascribe the over-burdening of Bering's plans to any one man, and for a foreign author, who but imperfectly understands the Russian literature of that period, to do so, would be more than foolish. Kiriloff, the secretary of the Senate, had great zeal for geographical explorations, and did all in his power to further the plans of Czar Peter. It has been proved that Bering's proposition was presented after a conference with Kiriloff, and that as long as he lived, he assisted Bering by word and deed. Furthermore, it seems probable that, in order to promote the exploration of Siberia, he prevented the Admiralty from sending Bering's expedition by sea south of Africa. However, it is undoubtedly a fact that Bering's plan reached its final proportions as a result of the discussions between Count Ostermann, the influential courtier and statesman, (who evidently landed in Russia in company with Bering in 1704), Soimonoff, an officer of the Senate, Kiriloff, and Golovin, chief of the Admiralty, and these men would hardly have consulted the opinions of Bering, who often and most emphatically disapproved of the additions that had been made to his plans. Moreover, as a result of the

---

* H. H. Bancroft, History of Alaska, p. 42, says: " The second Kamchatka expedition * * * * * was the most brilliant effort toward scientific discovery which up to this time had been made by any government."—Tr.

distrust which his first expedition inspired in Russia, he was in an insecure and unfortunate position. But he had reason to complain of other things. The gigantic task assigned to him demanded a despotic will endowed with dictatorial power. Bering lacked both, especially the latter.

The Senate exhausted itself in minute hints, directions, and propositions, instead of issuing definite orders concerning the necessary means. Unfortunately, too, numerous and exaggerated complaints had been made in regard to the suffering which Bering's first expedition had caused the Kamchatkans, and on this account the government was foolish enough to bind the chief's hands, while it simultaneously overloaded his shoulders. Through injudicious instructions he was made dependent upon his subordinates. It was bad enough that he was not to be permitted to take any decisive steps in Siberia without first consulting and coming to an agreement with the local authorities,— the governor of Tobolsk, the lieutenant-governor of Irkutsk, and the voivode of Yakutsk. On account of the great distances and the wretched roads such proceedings were well-nigh impossible. The government should have known that these authorities only under the most peremptory orders would comply with demands liable to exhaust the resources of the country and ruin the thinly-populated and poverty-stricken districts. This was, indeed, bad enough, but matters were much aggravated when the Senate ordered him to take action in all important questions, only after deliberation with his officers, and to refer every leading measure to a commission. Such a method of procedure

seems to us entirely incomprehensible. But Sokoloff,
who was himself a Russian naval officer, says on this
point, that the laws of the empire, which at that time
were in full force, required of every superior officer that
he should consult his subordinates before inaugurating
any new movement. In its instructions to Bering the
Senate expressly emphasized this decree of the law, and
it actually went so far as to order him, even in matters of
comparative unimportance, to seek the opinion of his
Academical associates, and always act in the strictest
accordance with his Russian colleague Chirikoff's propositions.

The chiefs of the different branches of the expedition
were of course subject to the same regulation. In this
way Bering was deprived of a sovereign chief's power and
authority, and it afforded him but little reparation that
the government gave him the power to reduce or promote
an officer,—only naval officers, however. Necessary regard for the needs of the service and for his own princi-
ples forbade him to use this weapon in that arbitrary
manner which alone could have neutralized the unfortunate influence of the government laws. Hence this
feature of his instructions, besides causing much delay,
became a source of the most incredible troubles and
aggravations, which, as we shall see later, laid him in his
grave on the bleak coasts of Bering Island.

Everything carefully considered, it could have surprised no one if the Northern Expedition had collapsed
in its very greatness, and it was without any doubt due to
Bering that this did not happen. In many respects
Bering was unqualified to lead such an expedition into a

barbarous country, surrounded as he was with incapable,
uneducated, and corruptible assistants, pestered by calum-
niators and secret or avowed enemies in every quarter, to
whom the government seemed more disposed to listen
than to him. More just than arbitrary, more considerate
than hasty, more humane than his position permitted, he
nevertheless had one important quality, an honest,
genuine, and tenacious spirit of perseverance, and this
saved the expedition from dissolution. The government
had sent him in pursuit of a golden chariot, and he
found more than the linch-pin. The realization, however, was far from that anticipated by the government.
Many of the projects of the original plan were but
partially accomplished, and others were not even attempted; but in spite of this, the results attained by
Bering and his associates will stand as boundary-posts
in the history of geographical discovery. Many of these
men sealed their work with their lives, and added a
luster to the name of Russia,* which later explorers have
maintained.

* Note 41.

CHAPTER IX.

IN the early part of the year 1733, the expedition began to leave St. Petersburg by detachments. It consisted of the chief Vitus Bering (his Russian name was Ivan Ivanovich Bering), Captains Spangberg and Chirikoff, eight lieutenants, sixteen mates, twelve physicians, seven priests, skippers, stewards, various apprentices, ship-carpenters, other workmen, soldiers and sailors,—in all about five hundred and seventy men. Of these, three officers and one hundred and fifty-seven men —a number which was greatly increased in Siberia— were assigned duty in the Arctic expedition, the remainder in the Pacific expeditions. In this estimate, the Academists, constituting an expedition of thirty or forty men, are not considered. The list of names of those engaged in these expeditions throws interesting light on Russian social relations of that period. Over half of the officers, many mates, and all of the physicians were foreigners. The Senate sought to inspire the zeal of the officers by large increase of salary and promotion in rank and service after a successfully completed expedition, but the rank and file were to be forced to a performance of their duties by threats of cruel punishments and a continued stay in Siberia. It had been the intention to recruit the expedition through the voluntary service of Russians, but the native officers showed but little inclination in this direction, and it was found necessary to fill the vacancies by draft. Van Haven assures us that Bering's expedition was looked upon in St. Petersburg as a mild sort of banishment.

The necessary instruments and some provisions were obtained in St. Petersburg. The naval officers were supplied with quadrants, thermometers, and nocturnals, the surveyors with astrolabes and Gunter's-chains, and the Academists were authorized to take from the library of the Academy all the works they needed, and, at the expense of the crown, to purchase such as the library did not contain. La Croyère carried with him a whole magazine of instruments. For presents to the natives two thousand rubles were appropriated. In N. Novgorod and Kazan some other necessaries were obtained, but the enormous ship-supplies and provisions, besides men, horses, barges and other river boats, were to be provided by the Siberian towns and country districts.

The Siberian authorities received orders to make great preparations. They were to buy venison, fish, and cod liver oil, erect light-houses and magazines along the Arctic coast, and dispatch commissions with large transports to the Pacific coast, so as to enable Bering to begin his work of discovery without delay. These preparations were to be followed by efforts toward the founding of various works, such as iron and salt works at Okhotsk, a smaller furnace at Yakutsk for the use of the expedition, and, through the utilization of the saccharine qualities of the "bear's claw," * a distillery was also to be established on the peninsula of Kamchatka. It is unnecessary to say that all of these propositions were buried in the Siberian government departments.

Calculations were made for a six years' expedition. The leaders of each branch of the expedition were authorized to repeat any unsuccessful adventure the succeeding summer. All were prepared for a long stay in the extreme northeast—many, indeed, remained there forever—hence, most of the officers, among them Bering and Spangberg, were accompanied by their wives and children. On this account the expedition seemed more than ever a national migration on a small scale.

The first start was made February 1, 1733. Spangberg, with some laborers and the heaviest marine stores, went directly to Okhotsk to expedite the ship-building on the Pacific coast. Lieutenant Ofzyn went to Kazan to collect supplies. Bering started out March 18, in order as quickly as possible to reach Tobolsk, whence the first Arctic expedition was to be sent out. In the course of the summer, the larger caravans arrived at this place. Simultaneously heavy supplies were brought in from West Siberia by Bering's men. Here, also, the construction of the vessel for the expedition, the shallop Tobol, was begun. Only the Academists were yet in St. Petersburg, where they were receiving the attention of the official world. At an audience, the Empress bade

* Note 7.

them farewell in the most solemn manner. She allowed them to kiss her hand, and assured them of
her most gracious favor. On the succeeding day, the
other members of the imperial family manifested similar sympathy. Then, however, the difficulties began.
That these heavily-laden gentlemen could not even in
St. Petersburg secure adequate means of transportation,
makes quite a comical impression. On this account
they were detained until late in August, and they
would no doubt have been unable to reach Siberia
in 1733, if Bering had not left for them in Tver a
conveniently equipped vessel, which carried them the
same autumn down the Volga to Kazan. They did
not reach Tobolsk, however, until January, 1734.
Bering, who was to be supplied by them with surveyors and instruments for his Arctic expedition, and
who could not, before their arrival, form an estimate
of the size of his river transports to be used in the
spring, was obliged repeatedly and very forcibly to
urge them to make haste. Here the disagreements
began, and were continued concerning petty affairs,
which history finds it unnecessary to dwell upon.

On May 2, 1734, the Tobol was launched amid the
firing of cannon, the blare of trumpets, and the merry
draining of goblets. The vessel had a keel of 70 feet,
was 15 feet wide, and 7 feet deep. It carried two masts,
some small cannon, and a crew of 56 men, among
them first mate Sterlegoff and two cartographers,
under the command of Lieut. Ofzyn. As the provin-
cial government had secured neither magazines nor provisions, nor attended to any other preparations on the

Arctic coast, the necessary supplies, which were to be stored north of Obdorsk, were loaded on four rafts, which, with a force of 30 men, accompanied Ofzyn. On May 14, he received his Admiralty instructions from Bering, and, saluted by cannon, the *First Arctic Expedition* stood up the Irtish for the Polar seas.

Five days later, Bering, with the main command and the Academists, left Tobolsk and took different routes for Yakutsk, which had been selected as the central point for the future enterprises of the expedition. In October, 1734, he arrived at this place, bringing with him a quantity of materials. The next spring, Chirikoff came with the greater part of the supplies, and during the year following, this dull Siberian city was the scene of no little activity. On his arrival, however, Bering found that no preparations whatever had been made for him. In spite of instructions and orders from the government, nothing had been done toward charting the Arctic coast or for the expediting of the heavily loaded transports on the way to Okhotsk. Nor did Bering find that the authorities were even kindly disposed toward him. Yet, in the course of the next six months, he had two large ships built for the Arctic expedition, and when his own supplies arrived by way of the central Siberian river-route, described in the first part of this work, these vessels, together with four barges, were equipped and furnished with provisions, and in June, 1735, were ready for a start. These two ships—the sloop Yakutsk, Lieut. Pronchisheff, first mate Chelyuskin, surveyor Chekin, and about fifty men, and the decked boat Irkutsk,

Lieut. Peter Lassenius, with a surveyor, first mate,
and also about fifty men—had most difficult tasks to
accomplish. The former was to cruise from the mouth
of the Lena, along the whole coast of the Taimyr
peninsula, and enter the mouth of the Yenisei. The
latter was to follow the Arctic coast in an easterly
direction to the Bering peninsula, cruise along its coast,
and ascertain the relative positions of Asia and America, and, if it was a geographical possibility, to sail
down to the peninsula of Kamchatka. He also had
instructions to find the islands off the mouth of the
Kolyma (the Bear Islands). From this it is evident
that Lassenius's expedition was of the greater geographical interest. Moreover, it had to do with one of
the main questions of Bering's whole activity—the discovery and charting of the North Pacific—and hence
it is not a mere accident that Bering selected for this
expedition one of his own countrymen, or that he assigned the charting of northeastern Asia and the discovery of America and Japan, to chiefs of Danish birth, Lassenius and Spangberg. Nothing is known of the earlier
life of Lassenius. In service he was the oldest of
Bering's lieutenants. Shortly before the departure
of the expedition, he was taken into the Russian fleet,
and Gmelin says of him, that he was an able and
experienced naval officer, volunteered his services to the
expedition, and began his work with intrepidity. All
attempts to trace his birth and family relations have
proved fruitless.

On the 30th of June, 1735, both expeditions left
Yakutsk, and thus the charting of the whole of the

Arctic coast of Siberia was planned and inaugurated by Bering himself. He could now apply all his energies to the Pacific expeditions. He constructed a multitude of river-craft, and erected barracks, magazines, winter-huts, and wharves along the river-route to Okhotsk. In the vicinity of Yakutsk he established an iron foundry and furnace, whence the various vessels were supplied with anchors and other articles of iron. In fact, he made this place the emporium for those heavy supplies that in the years 1735–36 were brought from South and West Siberia, and which later were to be sent to Okhotsk.

At Okhotsk the exiled Major-General Pissarjeff was in command. He had been sent there as a government official, with authority on the Pacific coast and in Kamchatka, to develop the country and pave the way for the expeditions to follow, by making roads and harbors, erecting buildings in Okhotsk, introducing agriculture,— in fact, make this coast fit for human habitation. The government had given him ample power, but as he accomplished nothing, he was succeeded by Captain Pavlutski as chief in Kamchatka, and Pissarjeff was reduced to a sort of harbor-master in Okhotsk. A command that had been sent to his assistance under first mate Bireff, he nearly starved to death; the men deserted and the town remained the same rookery as ever.

In this condition Spangberg found affairs in the winter of 1734–35. With his usual energy he had pushed his transports to Yakutsk in the summer preceding, and with the same boats he proceeded up the

Aldan and Maya, but winter came on and his boats were frozen in on the Yudoma. He started out on foot by the familiar route across the Stanovoi Mountains to Okhotsk, which place he reached after enduring great hardship and suffering; but even here he found no roof for shelter. He was forced to subsist on carcasses and roots, and not until the spring fishing began and a provision caravan sent by Bering arrived, did he escape this dire distress. In the early summer, Pissarjeff put in an appearance, and very soon a bitter and fatal enmity arose between these two men.

Spangberg was born in Jerne near Esbjerg in Jutland (Denmark), probably about the year 1698. He was the son of well-to-do parents of the middle class. In the Jerne churchyard there is still to be seen a beautiful monument on the grave of his brother, the "estimable and well-born Chr. Spangberg;" nothing else is known of his early life. In 1720, he entered the Russian fleet as a lieutenant of the fourth rank, and for a time ran the packet-boat between Kronstadt and Lübeck, whereupon he took part in Bering's first expedition as second in command. In 1732, for meritorious service on this expedition, he was made a captain of the third rank. He was an able, shrewd, and energetic man, a practical seaman, active and vehement, inconsiderate of the feelings of others, tyrannical and avaricious. He spoke the Russian language only imperfectly. His fame preceded him throughout all Siberia, and Sokoloff says that many thought him some general, *incognito*, others an

escaped convict. The natives of Siberia feared him
and called him Martin Petrovich Kosar, or in iron-
ical praise, "Batushka" (old fellow). He had many
enemies. Complaints and accusations were showered
upon him, but it would most certainly be wrong to
ascribe to them any great significance. Siberia is the
land of slander. All Russian officials were corruptible, and the honest men among those who stood
nearest to Peter himself could literally be counted
on one's fingers. While in Siberia, Spangberg is
said to have acquired the possession of many horses,
valuable furs, and other goods of which the authorities had forced the sale. When the Senate, after
his great voyage of discovery to Japan, had treated
him unjustly, he left Siberia arbitrarily in 1745,
and, without leave of absence, set out for St. Petersburg, where he was summoned before a court-martial and condemned to death; but this was finally
commuted to his being reduced to a lieutenant for
three months. He remained in the service and died,
in 1761, as a captain of the first rank. In Okhotsk
he was accompanied by his wife and son.*

But his opponent was a still more remarkable
man. Major-General Pissarjeff had been a favorite of
Peter the Great, director of the military academy,
and a high officer of the Senate. He had received a
careful education abroad, and moved in the very
highest circles of society. In a quarrel with Vice-
Chancellor Shafiroff, in 1722, however, he had incurred
Peter's wrath, whereupon he was for a time deprived

* Note 42.

of all official rank and banished to the Ladoga canal
as overseer of this great enterprise. Later he was
pardoned, but when, in 1727, he conspired against
Prince Menshikoff, he was deprived of everything,
knouted, branded, and then exiled to Siberia as a
colonist. After a series of vicissitudes he appeared,
in the capacity of harbor-master at Okhotsk, but the
government gave him no rank; he was not even permitted to cover his brand. This old man, made
vicious by a long and unjust banishment, became
Bering's evil spirit. In spite of his sixty or seventy
years, he was as restless, fiery and vehement in both
speech and action as when a youth, dissolute, corruptible, and slanderous—a false and malicious bab-
bler, a full-fledged representative of the famous Siberian "school for scandal." For six long years he
persecuted the expedition with his hatred and falsehoods, and was several times within an ace of overthrow-
ing everything. He lived in a stockaded fort a few
miles in the country, while Spangberg's quarters were
down by the sea, on the so-called Kushka, a strip
of land in the Okhota delta, where the town was to
be founded. The power of each was unrestrained.
Both were dare-devils who demanded an obedience
which foretold the speedy overthrow of each. Both
sought to maintain their authority through imprison-
ment and corporal punishment. Thus they wrangled
for a year, Pissarjeff, meanwhile, sending numerous
complaints to Yakutsk and St. Petersburg. But
Spangberg was not to be trifled with. In the fall
of 1736 he swore that he would effectually rid himself

of "the old scoundrel," who thereupon in all haste
fled to Yakutsk, where he arrived after a nine days'
ride, and filled the town with his prattling falsehoods,
to which, however, only the Academists seem to have
paid any attention.

Under circumstances where the local authorities did
everything in their power to hinder the development
of a district, it is only natural that in the settlement of
Okhotsk and the construction of the ships for the expedition but slow progress was made.   The enormous
stores which were necessary for six or eight sea-going
ships — provisions, cannon, powder, cables, hemp, can-
vas, etc., it would take two or three years to bring from
Yakutsk, a distance both long and tedious, and fraught
with danger.   The work, the superhuman efforts, the
forethought, and perseverance that Bering and his
men exhibited on these transporting expeditions on the
rivers of East Siberia have never been described or
understood, and yet they perhaps form the climax in
the events of this expedition, every page of the history of which tells of suffering and thankless toil.

In the middle of the 17th century, those Cossacks
that conquered the Amoor country had opened this
river navigation, and now Bering re-opened it.   The
stores were transported down the Lena, up the Aldan,
Maya, and Yudoma rivers, thence across the Stanovoi
Mountains, down the Urak, and by sea to Okhotsk.
These transportations at first employed five hundred
soldiers and exiles, and later more than a thousand.
The season is very short.   The rivers break up in the
early part of May, when the spring floods, full of

devastating drift-ice, rise twenty or thirty feet above
the average level and sweep along in their course
whole islands, thus filling the river-bed with trunks
of trees and sand, deluging the wild rock-encircled
valleys, so that navigation can not begin until the latter
part of May, again to be obstructed in August by
ice. The course was against the current, so the crew
had to walk along the rough and slippery banks and
tug the flat-bottomed barges up stream. In this way
they were usually able, during the first summer, to
reach the junction of the Maya and the Aldan (Ust
Maiskaya), where Bering built a pier and a number
of magazines, barracks, and winter-huts. Then the
next summer, the journey would be continued up the
Maya and into the Yudoma, which boils along through
an open mountain valley over rocks, stones, and water-
logged tree trunks. It has but two or three feet of
water, is full of sand-banks, with a waterfall here and
there and long rapids and eddies, — the so-called
"schiver." In such places the current was so strong
that thirty men were scarcely able to tug a boat
against it. Standing in water to their waists, the men
were, so to speak, obliged to carry the barges. The
water was very cauterizing, and covered their legs
and feet with boils and sores. The oppressive heat of
the day was followed by nights that were biting cold,
and when new ice was formed, their sufferings were
superhuman. In this manner Yudomskaya Krest
(Yudoma's Cross) was reached in August of the second
year. This place, where since the days of the Cossack expedition a cross had stood, Bering made an

intermediate station for the expedition.   Here were the
dwellings of two officers, a barrack, two earth-huts, six
warehouses, and a few other buildings and winter-
huts.   In these warehouses the goods were stored,
to be conveyed, in the following winter, on horseback
across the Stanovoi Mountains to the mountain stream
Urak, which, after a course of two hundred versts,
reaches the sea three miles south of Okhotsk.

For this part of the expedition, new winter-huts on
the Stanovoi Mountains, and magazines, river boats,
and piers on the Urak had to be built.   This river is
navigable only for a few days after the spring thaw.
Then it boils along at the rate of six miles an hour,
often making a trip down its course a dangerous one.
Losseff says that in this way, other things being favorable, Okhotsk was reached in three years.   The brief
account which has here been attempted gives but a
faint idea of the labor, perseverance, and endurance
requisite to make one of these expeditions.   Barges
and boats had to be built at three different places,
roads had to be made along rivers, over mountains,
and through forests, and piers, bridges, storehouses,
winter-huts and dwellings had to be constructed at
these various places.   Not only this.   They suffered
many misfortunes.   Boats and barges were lost, men
and beasts of burden were drowned, deserted, or were
torn to pieces by wolves,—and all these difficulties
Bering and his assistants overcame through their own
activity, without the support of the Siberian government, yes, in spite of its ill will, both concealed and
manifest.   In 1737, he reported to the Admiralty:

"Prior to our arrival at Yakutsk not a pood* of provisions had been brought to Okhotsk for us, nor had a single boat been built for the transportation. Nor did we find workmen or magazines at the landing places on the Maya and Yudoma rivers. The Siberian authorities have not taken a single step toward complying with the ukases issued by Her Royal Highness." And with justifiable self-esteem he adds: "We did all this. We built transports, we obtained workmen in Yakutsk, we conveyed our provisions to Yudomskaya Krest, and with superhuman efforts thence to the sea. At the mouths of the Maya and Yudoma, at the Cross, and at the Urak we erected storehouses and dwellings, in the Stanovoi Mountains several winter-huts, and on the Urak no less than seventy river boats, which have, in part, started for Okhotsk with provisions. Not until after the lapse of two years have I been able to induce the authorities in Yakutsk to appoint superintendents of transportation, and for this reason it was entirely impossible for me to depart for Okhotsk, unless I wanted to see the work of the whole expedition come to a complete standstill, bring upon my men the direst need, and force the whole enterprise into most ignominious ruin."

* A pood is thirty-six pounds.

CHAPTER X.

THE difficulties recounted in the preceding chapter are alone sufficient to justify Bering's nearly three years' stay in Yakutsk; but simultaneously many other duties demanded his attention. It does not come within the scope of this treatise to describe the investigations of the Academical branch of this enterprise,—to portray Müller's and Gmelin's services to botany, history, and geography; they are of interest here only in their relation to Bering. Especially in Yakutsk did these men give him much to attend to. It devolved upon him now to convey these gentlemen, in a manner fitting their station, up or down the Lena, now to send La Croyère to Lake Baikal or to the Arctic Ocean,—all of which was to be done in a country principally inhabited by nomadic tribes, with only here and there a Russian population where there were government officials, and with no other means of transportation than those secured for the occasion. In Yakutsk, where the Professors stayed a long time, their relations with Bering were very much strained, principally, it would seem, on account of their

exorbitant demands for convenience and luxury. Since
Bering would not and could not take upon himself to
transport them to Kamchatka as comfortably as he had
thus far conveyed them, especially not from Okhotsk, in
private and conveniently equipped vessels, and since the
Voivode likewise gave them but little hope of support,
both Gmelin and Müller made application for a release
from the expedition, and left to Krasheninnikoff and
Steller their principal task—the description of Kamchatka.

In the year 1736, moreover, very discouraging news was
received from the Arctic seas. Pronchisheff had been
obliged to go into winter quarters at Olenek, and Lassenius, who, August 2, had reached the rocky islet Stolb, in
the Lena delta, and on the 7th stood out of the mouth of
the Bykoff eastward, was driven by storm and ice into the
river Khariulakh, east of the Borkhaya Bay, where he
wintered, in a latitude of 71° 28'. The place was uninhabited, and he built from driftwood a winter-house 66 feet
long, making four apartments, with three fireplaces, and
a separate kitchen and bath-room. As Lassenius hoped
to be able to continue the expedition during the two
succeeding summers, the rations were made considerably
smaller.

November 6, the polar night began, and shortly afterwards nearly the whole crew were attacked by a deadly
scurvy, so violent that perhaps only Jens Munk* and his
fellow-sufferers on the Churchill River have experienced
anything worse. On the 19th of December Lassenius
died, and in the few succeeding months nearly all of his

---

*Munk was sent out by the Danish government in 1619 to search for a
Northwest passage.—TR.

officers and thirty-one of the crew, so that when assistance
from Bering arrived, only eight men were alive. Müller
and Gmelin say that the crew accused Lassenius of high
treason, and mutinied; but there is no documentary evidence of this. The report seems to have arisen through
a confounding of the name of Lassenius with that of the
deputy constable Rossęlius, who, on the 18th of November, 1735, was sent, under arrest, to Yakutsk. To fill
the vacancies caused by this terrible disease, Bering had to
send a whole new command—Lieut. Dmitri Laptjef, the
second mate Plauting, and forty-three men—to Khariulakh to continue the expedition. In addition to this,
two boats with provisions were sent to the mouth of the
Lena, and in 1737, before he himself departed for
Okhotsk, a shipload of provisions was sent to supply the
magazines on the Arctic coast. To these various tasks
Bering gave his personal attention.

In 1736–38 this great enterprise passed through a dangerous crisis. Several years had elapsed since the departure from St. Petersburg, three hundred thousand rubles
(over two hundred thousand dollars) had been expended
—an enormous sum at that time—and yet Bering could
not point to a single result. Lassenius was dead, his successor, D. Laptjef, had been unfortunate, Pronchisheff
had, in two summers of cruising, not been able to double
the Taimyr peninsula, Ofzyn was struggling in vain in
the Gulf of Obi, while Bering and Spangberg had not
begun their Pacific expeditions. The former had not
even reached the coast. The government authorities at
St. Petersburg were in the highest degree dissatisfied with
this seeming dilatoriness. The Senate sent a most earnest

appeal to the Admiralty to recall the expedition. Here was a situation that Bering's enemies thought favorable for their intrigues. The departments of the Admiralty were deluged with complaints and accusations. The Siberian authorities, of whom Bering so justly had complained, answered with counter-charges. He was not familiar with the country, they said; he made unreasonable demands, and did not know how to avail himself of means at hand. Pissarjeff told the government that Bering and Spangberg had undertaken this expedition into Siberia simply to fill their own pockets,—that they accepted bribes, carried on a contraband liquor traffic, and had already accumulated great wealth. The exiled naval officer, Kasanssoff, reported that there was entire lack of system in the enterprise; that everything was done at an enormous expenditure, and that nothing at all would be accomplished. Lieutenant Plauting, one of Bering's own officers, who had been reduced for neglect of duty, accused Bering of being arbitrary, extravagant, and fond of show at the expense of the government. He accused him, furthermore, of embezzlement on his first expedition, in 1725, and alleged that Bering's wife had returned to Russia with a fortune, and had in Yakutsk abducted two young women.*

History has not confirmed a single one of these charges. As for sacrifice, disinterestedness, and zeal, Bering not only rises far above his surroundings—which is, perhaps, not saying very much—but his character is clean and unsullied. Even so petty a person as Sokoloff, who, in other respects, does not spare him, has for his character

* Note 43.

unqualified praise. Nevertheless, all of these complaints and accusations caused Bering much trouble and vexation. The Admiralty, hard pressed by the Senate, found it difficult to furnish the necessary means for the continuation of the expedition, and treated Bering severely and unreasonably. It lacked the view which personal examination gives. It was beset with deceitfulness and circumvention, and its experiences led it to take the worst for granted. Hence, it sent Bering one message after the other reprehensive of his course. It threatened to fine him, to court-martial him, to reduce him, and, in 1737, it even went so far as to deprive him of his supplemental salary, which was withheld several years.* Bering defended himself with the bitterness of despair. In his reports he gave the most solemn assurances of his perseverance and fidelity to duty, and the most detailed accounts of all difficulties. He declared upon his honor that he was unable to see any other means or resources than those he had resorted to. He even appealed at last to the testimony of the chiefs of the various expeditions and all the subordinate officers. He was not believed. The Admiralty showed its lack of tact by letting Chirikoff investigate a series of charges against him. Furthermore, in spite of Bering's most urgent representations, Pissarjeff continued to retain his position in Okhotsk; and, although the government threatened the Siberian authorities with the sternest punishments, still the latter only very inactively participated in the work of the expedition.

Sokoloff gives a very repulsive picture of Bering's assistants. On account of the discomforts of the journey

* Note 44.

in this barbaric country, and under the pressure of ceaseless toil, a large number of the subordinates fell to drinking and committing petty thefts; and the officers, gathered as they were from all quarters of the world, are described as a band of gruff and unruly brawlers. They were always at sword's points. Pronchisheff and Lassenius, Chirikoff and Spangberg, the latter and Walton, Plauting, Waxel, Petroff and Endoguroff, were constantly wrangling, and at times most shameful scenes were enacted. Our Russian author is not adverse to giving Bering the principal blame for these dissensions which cast a gloom on this worthy undertaking and impaired the forces of the expedition. He repeatedly, and with much force, accuses him of being weak, and in the Imperial Marine this opinion seems yet to prevail.* Sokoloff says: "Bering was a well-informed man, eager for knowledge, pious, kind-hearted, and honest, but altogether too cautious and indecisive; zealous, persevering, and yet not sufficiently energetic; well liked by his subordinates, yet without sufficient influence over them, — too much inclined to allow himself to be affected by their opinions and desires, and not able to maintain strict discipline. Hence, he was not particularly well qualified to lead this great enterprise, especially in such a dark century and in in such a barbaric country as East Siberia." I do not doubt that we here find some of the elements of Bering's character, but Sokoloff was much more of an archivist than historian and student of human nature. _ In his long accounts he never succeeds, by means of describing any action or situation, in giving a psychological insight into

* Note 45.

Bering's character, and, as matters now stand, it is impossible to draw any tenable line between the errors and delays that were necessarily attendant upon such an overburdened enterprise, and those that were due to the possible inefficiency of the leader. By the authority of the Senate the expedition was not a monarchical unit under Bering, but a democratic association under an administrative chief. It is not difficult to collect from the literature of that day a series of expressions which accuse Bering of cruelty, imperiousness, and military arrogance. Of a hundred leaders in Bering's position ninety-nine would undoubtedly have thought it wise to leave the whole expedition. Steller has with far more delicacy and skill drawn the main lines of his mental physiognomy. "Bering was," he says, "a true and honest Christian, noble, kind, and unassuming in conduct, universally loved by his subordinates, high as well as low. Every reasonable person must admit that he always sought to perform the work entrusted to him to the best of his ability, although he himself confessed and often regretted that his strength was no longer sufficient for so difficult an expedition. He deplored the fact that the plans for the expedition had been made on a much larger and more extensive scale than he had proposed, and he expressed a desire that, on account of his age, he might be released from this duty and have the task assigned to some young and active Russian. As is well known, he was not naturally a man of quick resolve, but when one considers his fidelity to duty, his cheerful spirit of perseverance and careful deliberation, it is a question whether another, possessed of more fire and ardor, could have overcome the innumerable difficulties

of the expedition without having completely ruined those
distant regions; for even Bering, far removed from all
selfishness, was scarcely able in this regard to keep his
men in check. The only fault of which the brave man
can be accused, is that his too great leniency was as detri-
mental as the spirited and oftentimes inconsiderate conduct of his subordinates." It is undoubtedly true that
Bering was not fully equal to the task; but no one would
have been equal to this task. It is possible that his
humane conduct impaired the work of the expedition, but
this allegation still lacks proof, and Sokoloff, who wrote
his book as a vindication of Chirikoff against Von Baer's
sympathetic view of Bering, must be read with this reser-
vation. It is downright absurd to hold the leader responsible for the moral weaknesses of his officers, for he had
not chosen them, and was as dependent upon them as
they upon him. "It seems to me," says Von Baer,
"that Bering has everywhere acted with the greatest cir-
cumspection and energy, and also with the greatest for-
bearance. The whole expedition was planned on such a
monstrous scale that under many another chief it would
have foundered without having accomplished any results
whatever."

CHAPTER XI.

IN the summer of 1737, Bering changed his headquarters to Okhotsk, and in the course of the
autumn and winter, the greater part of his force was
transferred to the same place or distributed among the
various intermediate stations on the Yudoma, Maya,
and Urak. Spangberg and Bering built Okhotsk. At
the junction of the Okhota and the Kukhta, on one of
the narrow deltas, the so-called Kushka, they erected
a church for the expedition, a number of houses for
the officers, barracks, magazines, a large dock-yard,
and other buildings. The old stockaded fort, four
miles farther up in the country, was deserted. Around
the military center of the expedition the town gradually formed and rapidly grew to become the Russian
metropolis on the Pacific. It cost very great exer-
tions to make the place inhabitable. The site was a
long sand-bank deposit, threatened by inundations.
The climate was very unhealthy, — a cold, raw fog
almost continually hung over this region. The party
was pestered with fevers, and in this swamp it was
that Bering lost his health. "The place is new and
desolate," he writes. "We have sand and pebbles, no
vegetation whatever, and no timber in the vicinity.

Firewood must be obtained at a distance of four to five miles, drinking water one to two miles, while timber and joints for shipbuilding must be floated down the river twenty-five miles." But as a place for a dock-yard, as a harbor and haven of refuge for large ships, the location had such great advantages that these difficulties had to be overcome.

Spangberg's work had made the place. His men had worked clay, made tiles, and built houses, and when Bering arrived the ships Archangel Michael and Hope lay fully equipped in the harbor. Bering's old ships Fortuna and Gabriel had been repaired, and Spangberg lacked only an adequate supply of provisions to begin his expedition to Japan in the autumn of 1737.

But the provision transports, as usual, moved on very slowly and with great difficulty. In Okhotsk Spangberg's men were constantly in distress. They received only the rations of flour and rice authorized by law, and at long intervals some beef which Bering had bought in Yakutsk. On account of this scarcity of provisions Spangberg was obliged partially to stop work on the vessels. A part of his force was permitted to go a-fishing, a part were sent to the magazines in the country for their maintenance, while others were detached to assist in the work of transportation; hence it was with only a small force that he could continue work on the ships for the American voyage, the packet-boats St. Peter and St. Paul.

Sokoloff says: "Bering stayed three years in Okhotsk, exerting himself to the utmost in equipping expeditions, enduring continual vexations from the Siberian government — especially on account of Pissarjeff — and conducting frequent examinations and investigations into the quarrels and complaints of his subordinates. During all this time he was sternly and unreasonably treated by the Admiralty, which showered upon him threats and reproaches for slowness sluggishness, and disorder, for false reports and illtimed accounts." Even as late as 1740 the Senate made a proposition to discontinue the expedition, and only by calling attention to the enormous expenditures already made, which would in that case be completely wasted, was the Admiralty allowed to continue it. Bering was especially disheartened on account of Pissarjeff. The latter arrived at Okhotsk at the same time that Bering did, took up his abode in the old Ostrog (fort) and immediately began his malicious annoyances. His complaints and protests poured into headquarters at Okhotsk. "For a correspondence with him alone," writes Bering, "I might use three good secretaries. I find his foul-tongued criticism extremely offensive." He would capture Bering's men to give them a drubbing, while his own deserted him to join Bering, by whom they were kindly received. The new town and the Ostrog were two hostile camps. Finally Bering was compelled to make a sally to liberate his men. The intrepid Spangberg, entirely out of patience with Bering's leniency, said: "Why do you give yourself so much trouble about this old knave? Give me four men and the authority and I shall immediately put him under arrest."

Finally, in 1738, Spangberg found it possible to depart for Japan, and in two summer expeditions he charted the Kurile Islands, Yezo, and a part of the eastern coast of Nipon (Hondo), whereupon the cartography of this part of the globe assumed an entirely new appearance.

The expeditions to Japan, which employed four ships and several hundred men, had exhausted all the provisions in Okhotsk. It was again necessary to raise large supplies in West Siberia. A demand was made upon the government office in Tobolsk for 40,000 rubles. From the district of Verkhoiansk 50,000 poods of provisions, while in part from West Siberia and in part from the Admiralty 20,000 yards of cloth were received. From other very distant places oil, hemp, and other necessaries were obtained. The Admiralty despatched to Irkutsk and Yakutsk two naval officers, Lieutenants Tolbukhin and Larionoff, to superintend the transportation of these goods. The number of laborers was increased to a thousand, the roads were improved, more attendants were provided, the Siberian authorities exhibited more energy than before, new river-boats were constructed, and pack-horses were collected from a large radius of country; by these increased means it was possible to collect all necessaries in Okhotsk by 1740. In the month of June the ships for the American expedition, the St. Peter and the St. Paul, were launched. They were two-masters, 80 feet long, 22 feet wide, and $9\frac{1}{2}$ feet deep, rigged as brigs, each of 108 tons burden, carrying 14 two and three pound guns.

In the harbor and on the Sea of Okhotsk there was now quite a respectable fleet of eight or nine ships, all built by Bering. The Arctic coasts had been charted through his efforts. Spangberg had with great success completed his task, and had been sent by Bering to St. Petersburg to render a report. Bering's own force, which consisted of 166 men, besides 80 engaged in transporting, was now collected in Okhotsk. The astronomical department under La Croyère and the scientist Steller also arrived, and finally Bering had the satisfaction of seeing his worst enemy removed. In August, 1740, Pissarjeff was discharged, and poor Antoni Devier, first a cabin boy, then successively aid-de-camp, general, and chief of police in St. Petersburg — one of Peter the Great's most trusted companions in arms, but banished through the hatred of Men-shikoff — became his successor as harbor-master in Okhotsk.*

In the middle of August the packet-boats, the galley Okhotsk, and a double sloop containing the scientists were ready to sail for Kamchatka. Then Spangberg quite unexpectedly arrived. On his way home he had received a counter order. The authorities in St. Petersburg commanded him to repeat the expedition to Japan. This gave Bering some extra work in the way of letters and orders, so that the vessels under Bering's and Chirikoff's commands did not leave port until the 8th of September. They were supplied with provisions for twenty months, and their temporary destination was Avacha Bay on the

* Note 46.

east coast of Kamchatka, where they were to pass the
winter.   All the great enterprises which the government had instructed Bering to undertake had now
been begun.   In the following chapters will be found
a succinct account of the results of each.

PART III.

THE VARIOUS EXPEDITIONS.

CHAPTER XII.

THE Arctic expeditions made during the period from 1734 to 1743 have only in part any connection with the object of this work. These expeditions were, it is true, planned by Bering, and it was due to his activity and perseverance that they were undertaken. He secured vessels, men, and means, and had charge of the first unsuccessful attempt; he was responsible to the government, and in his zeal went just as far as his instructions would allow him. But his own special task soon taxed his time too heavily to permit him to assume charge of the Arctic expeditions. They were not carried out until several years after his departure from Yakutsk,— after he had ceased to be their leader. We have already shown Bering's important relation to them, something which has never before been done in West European literature. Hence our object, namely, to give Bering his dues, may therefore best be accomplished by giving a short account of the results achieved by these expeditions.

The world has never witnessed a more heroic geographical enterprise than these Arctic expeditions. In five or six different directions—from the Petchora, the Obi, the Yenesei, and the Lena—the unknown coasts of the Old

World were attacked.* For a whole decade these discoverers struggled with all the obstacles which a terrible
climate and the resources of a half developed country
obliged them to contend with. They surmounted these
obstacles. The expeditions were renewed, two, three,
yes, even four times. If the vessels were frozen in, they
were hauled upon shore the next spring, repaired, and the
expedition continued. And if these intrepid fellows were
checked in their course by masses of impenetrable ice,
they continued their explorations on dog sledges, which
here for the first time were employed in Arctic exploration. Cold, scurvy, and every degree of discomfort
wrought sad havoc among them, but many survived the
long polar winter in miserable wooden huts or barracks.
Nowhere has Russian hardiness erected for itself a more
enduring monument.

It was especially the projecting points and peninsulas
in this region that caused these explorers innumerable
difficulties. These points and capes had hitherto been
unknown. The crude maps of this period represented
the Arctic coast of Siberia as almost a straight line. It
was first necessary for the navigators to send cartographers
to these regions, build beacons and sea-marks, establish
magazines, collect herds of reindeer, which, partly as an
itinerant food supply, and partly to be used as an eventual

---

* Middendorff gives the following interesting outline of these expeditions:

From Petchora to the Obi:	From the Obi:	
Muravjoff and Pavloff.	Westward:	Eastward:
Malygin and Skuratoff.	Golovin.	Ofzyn.
		Minin.
		Koscheleff.
From the Yenesei:	From the Lena:	
Eastward:	Westward:	Eastward:
Minin.	Pronchisheff.	Lassenius.
	Chariton Laptjef.	Dmitri Laptjef.

means of conveyance, followed along the coast with the
vessels, while here and there, especially on the Taimyr
peninsula, small fishing stations were established for supplying the vessels.

In the summer of 1737 Malygin and Skuratoff crossed
the Kara Sea and sailed up the Gulf of Obi. In the
same year the able Ofzyn charted the coast between the
Obi and the Yenesei, but was reduced to the rank of a
common sailor, because in Berezov he had sought the
company of the exiled Prince Dolgoruki.

In the year previous, Pronchisheff all but succeeded
in doubling the Taimyr peninsula, and reached the
highest latitude (77° 29′) that had been reached by water
before the Vega expedition. But it was especially in the
second attempt, from 1738 to 1743, that the greatest
results were attained. The two cousins, Chariton and
Dmitri Laptjef, who were equipped anew and vested with
great authority, attacked the task of doubling the
Taimyr and Bering peninsulas with renewed vigor. By
extensive sledging expeditions, the former linked his
explorations to those undertaken by Minin and Sterlegoff
from the west, and his mate, Chelyuskin, in 1742,
planted his feet on the Old World's most northerly point,
and thus relegated the story of a certain Jelmerland, said
to connect northern Asia with Novaia Zemlia, to that
lumber-room which contains so many ingenious cartographical ideas. But even these contributions to science
were, perhaps, surpassed by those of Dmitri Laptjef. As
Lassenius's successor he charted, in three summers, the
Siberian coast from the Lena to the great Baranoff Cliff,
a distance of thirty-seven degrees. On this coast, toward

the last, he found himself in a narrow strait, from ten to
twenty yards wide, and he did not stop until there was
scarcely a bucketful of water between the polar ice and
the rocky shore. But Cape Schelagskii, on the northeast
coast, where Deshneff a century before had shown the
way, he did not succeed in doubling.

As a result of the labors of this great Northern
Expedition, the northern coast of the Old World
got substantially the same cartographical outline that
it now has. The determinations of latitude made by
the Russian officers were very accurate, but those of
longitude, based on nautical calculations, were not so
satisfactory. Their successors, Wrangell, Anjou, Middendorff, and even Nordenskjöld, have therefore found
opportunity to make corrections of but minor importance, especially in regard to longitude.

But it is necessary to dwell a little longer on
these expeditions. Their principal object was not so
much the charting of northern Siberia as the discovery and navigation of the Northeast passage.
From this point of view alone they must be considered. This is the connecting thought, the central
point in these scattered labors. They were an indi-
rect continuation of the West European expeditions
for the same purpose, but far more rational than
these. For this reason Bering had, on his expedition of reconnoissance (1725–30), first sought that
thoroughfare between the two hemispheres without
which a Northeast and a Northwest passage could
not exist. For this reason also he had, on his far-
sighted plan, undertaken the navigation of the Arctic

seas, where this had not already been done by Deshneff, and for this same reason the Admiralty sought carefully to link their explorations to the West European termini, on the coast of Novaia Zemlia as well as Japan. Moreover, the discovery of a Northeast passage was the *raison d'être* of these expeditions.

This alone promised the empire such commercial and political advantages that the enormous expenditures and the frightful hardships which these expeditions caused Siberia, might be justified. For this reason the government, summer after summer, drove its sailors on along the Taimyr and Bering peninsulas; for this reason, in 1740, it enjoined upon D. Laptjef to make a last attempt to double northeast Asia from Kamchatka, and this would undoubtedly have been accomplished if the unfortunate death of Bering had not occurred shortly after;* and for this reason, also, the government caused the charting of the coast by land after all nautical attempts had miscarried.

Any extended documentary proof of the correctness of this view must be considered unnecessary. The instructions expressly state the object of the expedition: to ascertain with certainty whether vessels could find a passage or not. Müller says the same. Scholars like Middendorff, Von Baer, and Dr. Petermann look upon these expeditions from the same standpoint, and have seen fit to give them the place of honor among all the geographical efforts in the Northeast passage.† Some Swedish scholars alone have found it necessary to maintain a different view. Dr. A. Stuxberg and Prof. Th.

* Note 47.   † Note 48.

M. Fries in Upsala have published accounts of the history of the Northeast passage, in which not a word about these expeditions is found. Between the days of Vlaming and Cook, from 1688 until 1778, they find nothing to be said of explorations in this part of the world, and the charting of these waters does not, in their opinion, seem to have any connection with the history of the Northeast passage. Prof. Fries attempts to justify this strange method of treatment by the assertion that these expeditions did not seek the navigation of the Northeast passage, and did not undertake to sail a ship from the Atlantic to the Pacific. But what authority, what historical foundation, have such assertions? Simply because the Russians parceled out this work and went at it in a sensible manner; because they did not loudly proclaim their intention to sail directly from the Dwina to Japan; because they had been instructed by the visionary and fatal attempts of West Europe,—yes, one is almost tempted to say, just because these Russian expeditions alone are of any importance in the early history of the passage, the Swedish historians pass them by; Prof. Fries has even ventured the assertion that the discovery of the Northeast passage by these Russian expeditions, one hundred and thirty-seven years before Nordenskjöld, is a discovery hitherto unsurmised by anyone but the author of this work. I am not disposed to wrangle about words, and still less to interfere with anyone's well-earned privileges. By the discovery of the Northeast passage, I understand that work of geographical exploration, that determination of the distribution of land and water along the northern boundary of the Old World, that traversing and charting of the coast which showed the existence of the passage, but not the nautical utilization of it. This is the European interpretation of this question. In any other sense McClure did not discover the Northwest passage. If it is permissible to speak of the discovery of the Northeast passage after the time of Bering and the Great Northern Expedition, it is equally permissible to speak of the discovery of the Northwest passage after the time of the great English expeditions. If some future Nordenskjöld should take it into his head to choose these waters as the scene of some great nautical achievement, McClure, according to Prof. Fries's historical maxims, could not even find a place in the history of this passage, for it was not his object to sail a ship around the north of the New World. I very much doubt, however, that the Professor would in such a case have the courage to apply his maxims.

Nor does Baron Nordenskjöld concede to the Great Northern Expedition a place in the history of the Northeast passage. The "Voyage of the Vega" is an imposing work, and was written for a large public, but even the author of this work has not been able to rise to an unbiased and just estimate of his most important predecessors. His presentation of the subject of Russian explorations in the Arctic regions, not alone Bering's work and that of the Great Northern Expedition, but also Wrangell's, Lütke's, and Von Baer's, is unfair, unsatisfactory, inaccurate, and hence misleading in many respects. Nordenskjöld's book comes with such overpowering authority, and has had such a large circulation, that it is one's plain duty to point out palpable errors. Nordenskjöld is not very familiar with the literature relating to this subject. He does not know Berch's, Stuckenberg's, or Sokoloff's works. Middendorff's and Von Baer's clever treatises he uses only incidentally. He has restricted himself to making extracts from Wrangell's account, which in many respects is more than incomplete, and does not put these expeditions in the right light. It is now a couple of generations since Wrangell's work was written, which is more a general survey than an historical presentation. While Nordenskjöld devotes page after page to an Othere's, an Ivanoff's, and a Martinier's very indifferent or wholly imaginary voyages around northern Norway, he disposes of the Great Northern Expedition, without whose labors the voyage of the Vega would have been utterly impossible, in five unhappily written pages. One seeks in vain in his work for the principal object of the Northern Expedition,— for the leading idea that made these magnificent enterprises an organic whole, or for a full and just recognition of these able, and, in some respects, unfortunate men, whose labors have so long remained without due appreciation. In spite of Middendorff's interesting account of the cartography of the Taimyr peninsula, Nordenskjöld does not make the slightest attempt to explain whether his corrections of the cartography of this region are corrections of the work of Laptjef and Chelyuskin, or of the misrepresentations of their work made by a later age.

About the charting of Cape Chelyuskin he says: "This was done by Chelyuskin in 1742 on a new sledging expedition, the details of which are but little known;

evidently because until the most recent times there has been a doubt in regard to Chelyuskin's statement that he had reached the most northerly point of Asia. After the voyage of the Vega, however, there can no longer be any doubt." *

The truth is, ever since 1843,† when Middendorff published the preliminary account of his expedition to the Taimyr peninsula, no doubt has prevailed that all who are familiar with Russian literature, or even with German literature, on this subject, have long since been convinced of the fact that the most northern point of Asia was visited and charted a century and a half ago,— that the details of Chelyuskin's expedition, so far from being unknown, are those parts of the work of the Northern Expedition which have been most thoroughly investigated and most often presented. Nordenskjöld's recognition of Chelyuskin's work comes thirty-eight years too late; it has already been treated with quite a different degree of thoroughness than by the few words expended on it in the "Voyage of the Vega." In 1841, Von Baer accused Chelyuskin of having dishonestly given the latitude of the most northerly point of Asia, and these charges Nordenskjöld prints as late as 1881 without any comment whatever. If he had only seen Von Baer's magazine for 1845 ‡ he would there have found the most unreserved retraction of them and most complete restitution to Chelyuskin on the part of Von Baer, and would thus have escaped ascribing to a man opinions which he renounced a generation ago. Middendorff is likewise very painstaking in presenting the history of these measurements,

*Note 49.   †Note 50.   ‡Note 51.

and is open and frank in his praise. He says: "In the spring of 1742 Chelyuskin crowned his work by sailing from the Khatanga River around the eastern Taimyr peninsula and also around the most northerly point of Asia. He is the only one who a century ago had succeeded in reaching and doubling this promontory. The fact that among many he alone was successful in this enterprise, must be attributed to his great ability. On account of his perseverance, as well as his careful and exact measurements, he stands preëminent among seamen who have labored in the Taimyr country." And furthermore, in 1785, Sokoloff published a very careful and extensive account of these labors, together with an extract from Chelyuskin's diary relating to the charting of the Taimyr peninsula, which later was published in German by Dr. Petermann.* The difference in latitude of the northern point of the Taimyr peninsula as determined by Chelyuskin and by Nordenskjöld is scarcely three minutes.†

* Note 52.

† In his review of my book in the *Journal of the American Geographical Society*, XVII., p. 288, Baron Nordenskjöld says: "Mr. Lauridsen has devoted nearly two pages to showing that I am wrong in what I have said of Chelyuskin—that 'up to a recent date the statement that he really did reach the northern point of Asia was doubted.' But I had certainly the right to say this. If a person in 1742 performed one of the heroic deeds of geography without having received any acknowledgment for it in his lifetime, and if the best authorities in this person's own country a century later still considered him an impostor, I was surely justified in giving the above-quoted opinion in 1880, in spite of the fact that two eminent geographical authorities have withdrawn their charges. Moreover, is it really the case that Sokoloff's and Von Baer's later writings made it impossible to revive the old charge? He who can assert this must be but slightly acquainted with the history of geography, and with that of Siberian geography above all." In a note Nordenskjöld adds: "Previous to the departure of the Vega from Sweden, I received a letter from an unknown well-wisher to our voyage, cautioning me not to put too much faith in the Chelyuskin exploration story, as the writer of the letter

CHAPTER XIII.

THE DISCOVERY OF THE KURILE ISLANDS AND JAPAN FROM THE NORTH.

THE men that took part in these early Russian explorations have not yet received their just dues. Not one of them, however, needs rehabilitation so much as Spangberg. He is entitled to an independent place in geographical history, but has been completely barred out. O. Peschel and Prof. Ruge know him as Bering's principal officer, but not as the discoverer of the Kurile Islands and Japan from the north. And yet, just this was his task. He was to sail from Kamchatka to Nipon, chart the Kurile Islands, link the Russian explorations to the West European cartography of northern Japan, and investigate the geography of the intervening region,— especially the cartographical monsters which in the course of a century of contortion had developed from De Vries's intelligent map of East Yezo, Iturup (Staaten Eiland) and Urup (Kompagniland). We have already

considered it fictitious." To the Baron's criticism I shall simply remark: I have shown in the text that when he wrote the "Voyage of the Vega" he was not familiar with the latest works on this question. Hence he has been entirely unable to decide whether the old doubts concerning Chelyuskin's results could be revived or not. I appeal to all students of these finer points in the history of geography, who will certainly agree with my statement that the Baron in this question has absolutely no other support than that of an anonymous letter!—*Author's Note to American Edition.*

spoken of these geographical deformities, which assumed
the most grotesque forms, and were at that time accepted
by the scientific world. The version of the brothers
De l'Isle, which perhaps was the most sober, may be
seen from Map II. in the appendix.

By Strahlenberg (1730) and by Bellin and Charlevoix
(1735), highly respected names among scholars of that
day, Kamchatka and Yezo were represented as forming a
great continent separated by narrow sounds from Japan,
which was continued on the meridian of Kamchatka
and Yezo, and from an eastern chain of islands — Staaten
Eiland and Kompagniland — that seemed to project into
the Pacific in the form of a continent.

Kiriloff, who was familiar with Bering's map of eastern Asia, and made use of it, and who knew of the
most northerly Kuriles, made the necessary corrections
in his general map of Russia (1734), but retained, in
regard to Yezo and Japan, a strangely unfortunate com-
position of Dutch and Strahlenberg accounts, and put
Nipon (Hondo) much too far to the east. In these
cartographical aids Spangberg found only errors and
confusion, and he got about the same kind of assistance from his real predecessors in practical exploration.
Peschel tells that Ivan Kosyrefski, in the years 1712–13,
thoroughly investigated the Kurile chain ; there is, however, but little truth in this. Peschel gives G. F.
Müller as his authority and refers to his book, but the
latter says explicitly on this point: "All of Kosyrefski's
voyages were confined to the first two or three Kuriles ;
farther than this he did not go, and whatever he tells
of beyond them was obtained from the accounts of

others. " It is possible that Müller's judgment is a trifle
one-sided, but it is nevertheless certain that Kosyrefski's
description of the Kuriles is based on his own explorations only in a very slight degree, and that he by no
means deserves the place that Peschel and Ruge have
accorded him. Nor did Lushin's and Yevrinoff's expedition in the summer of 1721 get very far—scarcely
beyond the fifth or sixth island—and with them, until
Spangberg appeared on the scene, Russian explorations
in this quarter were at a standstill.

The expedition to Japan (1738) was undertaken with
three ships. Spangberg and Petroff sailed the one-
masted brig, the Archangel Michael, Lieutenant Walton
and first mate Kassimiroff the three-masted double sloop
Hope, and Second-Lieutenant Schelting had Bering's
old vessel, the Gabriel. The Michael had a crew of
sixty-three, among them a monk, a physician, and an
assayer, and each of the other two ships had a crew of
forty-four. The flotilla left Okhotsk on the 18th of June,
1738, but was detained in the Sea of Okhotsk by ice,
and did not reach Bolsheretsk until the early part of
July. From here, on the 15th of July, Spangberg
departed for the Kuriles to begin charting.

The Kurile chain, the thousand islands or Chi-Shima,
as the Japanese call them, is 650 kilometers long. These
islands are simply a multitude of crater crests which
shoot up out of the sea, and on that account make navigation very difficult. The heavy fog, which almost continually prevails here, conceals all landmarks. In the
great depths, sounding afforded little assistance, and,
furthermore, around these islands and through the

narrow channels there are heavy breakers and swift
currents.

For nearly a century after Spangberg, these obstacles
defied some of the world's bravest seamen. Captain
Gore, who was last in command of Cook's ships, was
obliged to give up the task of charting this region; La
Pérouse succeeded in exploring only the Boussale channel; the fogs forced Admiral Sarycheff (1792) to give
up his investigations here; Captain Broughton (1796)
was able to circumnavigate only the most southerly
islands, without, however, succeeding in giving a correct representation of them; and not until the early
part of this century did Golovnin succeed in charting
the group more accurately than Spangberg. All of
these difficulties were experienced in full measure
by Spangberg's expedition. In constant combat with
fogs, swift currents, and heavy seas along steep and
rocky coasts, he had, by the 3d of August, 1738, circumnavigated thirty-one islands (our maps have not
nearly so large a number), and at a latitude of 45° 30'
he reached the large island Nadeshda, (the Kompagniland of the Dutch, Urup), but, as he could nowhere
find a place to anchor, and as the nights were growing
dark and long, the ship's bread running short, and the
crew for a long time having been on half rations, he
turned back, and reached Bolsheretsk on the 17th of
August. Lieutenant Walton, who had parted company
with his chief and had sailed as far down as 43° 30'
north latitude, thus reaching the parallel of Yezo,
arrived a few days later. As well as the other chiefs of
these expeditions, Spangberg had authority, without a

renewed commission, to repeat the expedition the following summer ; hence the winter was spent in preparations for it. So far as it was possible to do so, he sought to provision himself in Kamchatka, and, especially for reconnoitering the coast, he built of birchwood an eighteen-oared boat called the Bolsheretsk.

On the 21st of May, 1739, he again stood out to sea with all four ships, and on the 25th of the same month he reached Kurile Strait, and from here sailed south southeast into the Pacific to search for Gamaland and all the legendary group of islands which appeared on De l' Isle's map. This southerly course, about on the meridian of Kamchatka, he kept until the 8th of June, reaching a latitude of 42°. As he saw nothing but sea and sky, he veered to the west south-west for the purpose of "doing the lands" near the coast of Japan. Walton, who, in spite of Spangberg's strictest orders, was constantly seeking to go off on his own tack, finally, on the 14th of June, found an opportunity to steal away and sail in a south-westerly direction. In different latitudes, but on the same day, the 16th of June, both discovered land. Walton followed the coast of Nipon down to latitude 33°, but Spangberg confined his explorations to the region between 39° and 37° 30' N. The country was very rich. A luxuriant vegetation — grape vines, orange trees and palms—decked its shores. Rich fields of rice, numerous villages, and populous cities were observed from the vessel. The sea teemed with fish of enormous size and peculiar form, and the currents brought them strange and unknown plants. The arrival of the ships caused great excitement among the natives, beacons burned

along the coast all night, and cruisers swarmed about
them at a respectful distance. On the 22d, Spangberg
cast anchor one verst from shore, and sought to commu-
nicate with them. The Japanese brought rice, tobacco,
various kinds of fruits and cloths, which, on very reasonable terms, they exchanged for Russian wares. They
were very polite, and Spangberg succeeded in obtaining
some gold coins, which, however, he found were described
by Kæmpfer. Several persons of high rank visited him
in his cabin and attempted to explain to him, by the aid
of his map and globe, the geography of Japan and Yezo.
As his instructions enjoined upon him the most extreme
cautiousness, and as on the following day he found himself surrounded by eighty large boats, each with ten or
twelve men, he weighed anchor and stood out to sea in a
northeasterly direction.

It was Spangberg's purpose to chart the southern part
of the Kurile Islands, and, as will be seen from his chart,*
he sought to accomplish his task, and thus complete his
work of 1738. The casual observer will, however, find
this map unsatisfactory and inaccurate, and will not
only be quite confused in viewing these islands so pro-
miscuously scattered about, and which seemingly do
not correspond with the actual geography of this region
as known to us, but he will even be inclined to suspect
Spangberg of gross fraud. This is certainly very unjust,
however, and after a careful study of a modern map, I
venture the following opinion on this subject: In order
to be able to understand his chart and course, the most
essential thing necessary is simply to determine his first

*See Appendix.

place of landing in the Kuriles, the island Figurnyi, and
to identify it with its present name. He discovered this
island on the 3d of July. Müller says that, according to
the ship's journal, it is in latitude 43° 50′ N., and in spite
of the fact that Spangberg's determinations in longitude,
based on the ship's calculations, were as a rule somewhat
inaccurate, which in a measure is shown by Nipon's being
located so far west, he is nevertheless in this case right.
Figurnyi is the island Sikotan and has the astronomical
position of this island on the chart (according to Golovnin
43° 53′ N. and 146° 43′ 30″ E.). This opinion is corroborated by a map of the Russian discoveries published at
St. Petersburg in 1787, and by Captain Broughton, who
described the island in the fall of 1796, and gave it the
name of Spangberg's Island, in honor of its first discoverer. With this point fixed, it is not difficult to
understand and follow Spangberg.

Spangberg labored under very unfavorable circumstances. It rained constantly, the coast was enveloped in
heavy fogs, and at times it was impossible to see land at
a distance of eight yards. From Figurnyi he sailed
southwest, but under these difficult circumstances he
took the little islands of Taroko and the northern point
of Yezo to be one continuous coast (Seljonyi, the green
island), and anchored at the head of Walvisch bay, his
Bay of Patience. From here he saw the western shore of
the bay, reached its farthest point, Cape Notske, and
discovered the peninsula of Sirokot and parts of the
island Kumashiri, which he called Konosir and Tsyn-
trounoi respectively; but, as he turned from Cape Notske
and sailed east into the Pacific, between Sikotan and the

Taroko Islands, he did not reach the Kurile Islands themselves, and only the most northerly island in the group
of the "Three Sisters" may possibly be the southern
point of Iturup. He then proceeded along the eastern
coast of Yezo, took the deep bay of Akischis as a strait
separating Seljonyi and Konosir, then crossed in a southerly direction the large bay on the central coast of Yezo,
without seeing land at its head, to Cape Jerimo (his
Matmai), and had thus navigated the whole east coast of
Yezo; but on account of the heavy fog, which prevented
him from seeing the exact outline of the coast, he made
three islands of Yezo: Matmai, Seljonyi and Konosir. In
1643, De Vries had in his map linked a number of islands
together, making one stretch of country called Jeco, and
now Spangberg had gone to the opposite extreme.

These explorations engaged Spangberg from the 3d to
the 25th of July. He several times met inhabitants of
North Yezo, the Aïno people, whose principal characteristics he has fully described, but as his men were suffering from scurvy, causing frequent deaths among them
(by August 29, when he arrived at Okhotsk, he had
lost thirteen, among them the physician), he resolved to
turn at Cape Jerimo, and on his return trip keep his
course so close to the Kuriles that he might strike the
extreme points of De l'Isle's Jeço, all of Kompagniland,
and the most westerly parts of Gamaland.

Spangberg's explorations were far from exhaustive.
He but partly succeeded in lifting the veil that so
persistently concealed the true outline of this irregularly
formed part of the globe. His reconnoissance was to
ascertain the general oceanic outline of these coasts.

His charting of Yezo and Saghalin was left to a much later day,—to La Pérouse, to Krusenstern, Golovnin, and others. But Spangberg's expedition nevertheless marks great progress in our geographical knowledge, for not only did he irrevocably banish the cartographical myths of that region, and, on the whole, give a correct representation of the Kurile islands clear to Iturup, the next to the last of them, but he also determined the position of North Japan, and fully accomplished his original task, namely, to show the Russians the way to Japan, and thus add this long disputed part of the Northeast passage to the other explorations for the same purpose.

As was the case with that of all of his colleagues, so Spangberg's reputation suffered under the violent administrative changes and that system of suppression which later prevailed in Russia. His reports were never made public. The Russian cartographers made use of his chart, but they did not understand how to fit judiciously his incomplete coast-lines to those already known, or to distinguish right from wrong. They even omitted the course of his vessel, thus excluding all possibility of understanding his work. Hence Spangberg's chart never reached West Europe, and Cook found it necessary to reinstate him as well as Bering.* After that the feeling was more favorable, and Coxe,† for instance, used his representation of the Kuriles; but new and better outlines of this region appeared about this time, and Spangberg again sank into complete oblivion.

Spangberg's safe return was a bright spot in the history of the Great Northern Expedition, and Bering

* Note 53. † Note 54.

was very well satisfied with the results. He permitted
him and his crew to go to Yakutsk to obtain rest, and
ordered him to return to St. Petersburg the next spring
to render in person an account of the results of the
expedition. His preliminary report, sent in advance,
received considerable attention in the cabinet of the
Empress, and caused much talk in the leading circles of
the capital. While in Yakutsk, he received orders to
travel day and night to reach St. Petersburg. Meanwhile, however, his old enemy Pissarjeff had also been
active. Surreptitiously, especially from Walton, who
was constantly at enmity with his chief, he had obtained
some information concerning the expedition and had
reported to the Senate that Spangberg had not been in
Japan at all, but off the coast of Corea. This assertion
he sought to prove by referring to pre-Spangberg maps,
which, as we have noted, placed Japan eleven or twelve
degrees too far east, directly south of Kamchatka. This
gossip was credited in the Senate, and a courier was
dispatched to stop Spangberg. At Fort Kirinsk, on the
Lena, in the summer of 1740, he received orders to
return to Okhotsk and repeat his voyage to Japan, while
a commission of naval officers and scholars betook themselves to investigate the matter. These wise men, after
several years of deliberation, came to the conclusion that
Walton had been in Japan, and that Spangberg most
probably had been off the coast of Corea. In the
summer of 1742, he started out on his third expedition to
Japan, but as this was a complete failure, undoubtedly
due to Spangberg's anger on account of the government's
unjust and insane action, and as it has no geographical
significance, we shall give it no further consideration.

CHAPTER XIV.

WE left Bering when, in 1740, he was about to depart from the harbor of Okhotsk with the St. Peter and the St. Paul, two smaller transports, and a vessel to convey the scientists, Steller and La Croyère, to Bolsheretsk. The objective point of the main expedition was Avacha Bay, on the eastern coast of Kamchatka. The excellent harbors here had been discovered by Bering's crew a couple of years previous. He had now sent his mate, Yelagin, to chart the bay, find a sheltered harbor there, and establish a fortified place of abode on this coast. This work Yelagin completed in the summer of 1740, and when in the latter part of September the packet boats entered Avacha Bay, they found, in a smaller bay on the north side, Niakina Cove, some barracks and huts. A fort was built in the course of the winter and the pious Bering had a church built and consecrated to St. Peter and St. Paul, thus founding the present town of Petropavlovsk. The place rapidly became the most important and pleasant town of the peninsula, although that is not saying much. In 1779, the place was still so insignificant that Cook's officers searched long in vain for it with their field-glasses, but finally discovered about thirty huts on that point which shelters the harbor. In the middle of this century it had about a thousand inhabitants, but since the sale of Russian America, Bering's town has been hopelessly on the decline. At present it has scarcely 600 inhabitants and is of importance only to the fur trade.

Its first permanent inhabitants were brought from the forts on the Kamchatka, and in the course of the autumn there arrived from Anadyrskoi Ostrog a herd of reindeer to supply the command of over two hundred men with food, and thus spare other stores. This was very necessary, for although Bering had left Okhotsk with nearly two years' provisions, one of the ships, through the carelessness of an officer, stranded in crossing the Okhotsk bar, and the cargo, consisting of the ship's bread for the voyage to America, was destroyed and could not immediately be replaced. Some lesser misfortunes in Avacha Bay further diminished the stores, and hence, in the course of the winter, Bering found it necessary to have large supplies brought across the country from Bolsheretsk. The distance is about one hundred and forty miles, and as nothing but dogs could be procured, the natives were gathered from the remotest quarters of the peninsula to accomplish this work of transportation. The Kamshadales disliked journeys very much. They had already suffered terribly under the misrule of the Cossacks. They were treated cruelly, and many died of overwork and want, and the rest lost patience. The tribes in the vicinity of Tigil revolted. The Cossack chief Kolessoff, who was constantly drunk, neglected to superintend the transportation, and as a result, much was injured or ruined. Some of these supplies arrived too late to be used for the expedition. Bering's original plan was to spend two years on this expedition. He was to winter on the American coast, navigate it from 60° N. latitude to Bering Strait, and then return along the coast of Asia. But this had to be abandoned.

In May, 1741, when the ice broke up, he could supply his ships with frugal, not to say very poor, provisions, for only five and a half months. Moreover, his ship's stores and reserve rigging were both incomplete and inadequate. Bering's powers of resistance now began to wane. After eight years of incessant trouble and toil, after all the accusations and suspicions he had undergone, he was now forced to face the thought of an unsatisfactory conclusion of his first voyage, at least. Besides, Spangberg's fate could not but have a very depressing influence, for it told Bering and his associates that even with the best of results it would hardly be possible to overcome the prejudices of the government authorities or their lack of confidence in the efforts of the new marine service. Undoubtedly it was such thoughts as these that swayed Bering and Chirikoff, when, on the 4th of May, they called the ship's council to consider the prospective voyage (the proceedings are not known). Although both, as well as the best of their officers, were of the opinion that America* was to be sought in a direction east by north from Avacha, and in spite of the fact that they

* Note 55.

were both familiar with Gvosdjeff's discovery of the American coast of Bering Strait (1732), and that their observations during the course of the winter had amply corroborated Bering's earlier opinion, they nevertheless allowed themselves to be prevailed upon to search first in a southeasterly direction for the legendary Gamaland. And thus the lid of Pandora's box was lifted.

This fatal resolution was due principally to the brothers De l'Isle, and, as this name is most decisively connected with Bering's life and renown, we must say a few words about these brothers. The elder and more talented, Guillaume De l'Isle, undoubtedly represented the geographical knowledge of his day, but he died as early as 1726. He came in personal contact with the Czar during the latter's visit in Paris, and corresponded with him afterwards. His maps were the worst stumbling blocks to Bering's first voyage. The younger brother, Joseph Nicolas, on the other hand, was called to Russia in 1726, on his brother's recommendation, and was appointed chief astronomer of the newly founded Academy. In this position he was for twenty-one years engaged upon the cartography of the great Russian empire. Under his supervision the atlas of the Academy appeared in 1745, and it was supposed that he carried very valuable geographical collections with him to Paris in 1747. But if this was the case, he did not understand how to make proper use of them, and, as it is, he is of no geographical importance. When he went to Russia, he took with him, without special invitation, his elder brother, Louis, and did everything to secure him a scientific position in the country. Louis seems to have been

an amiable good-for-nothing, who highly prized a good
table and a social glass, but cared as little as possible
for scientific pursuits.   When, as a young man, he
studied theology in Paris, his father found it necessary
to send him to Canada, where he assumed his mother's
name, La Croyère, and for seventeen years lived a soldier's wild life, until his brothers, on the death of the
father, recalled him from his exile.   In St. Petersburg
his brother instructed him in the elements of astronomy,
sent him upon a surveying expedition to Lapland, and
finally secured him a position as chief astronomer of
Bering's second expedition.   This was a great mistake.
Louis de l'Isle de la Croyère very unsatisfactorily filled
his position.   His Academic associates Müller and Gmelin
had no regard for him whatever, and hence under the
pressure of this contempt, and as a result of this irregular
and protracted life in a barbaric country, La Croyère,
having no native power of resistance, sank deeper and
deeper into hopeless sluggishness.   His astronomical
determinations in Kamchatka are worthless.   His Russian assistants, especially Krassilnikoff, did this part of
the work of the expedition.

As early as 1730, Bering, as we have seen, came into
unfortunate relations with Joseph De l'Isle, and this state
of affairs afterwards grew gradually worse.   In 1731, the
Senate requested the latter to construct a map of the
northern part of the Pacific in order to present
graphically the still unsolved problems for geographical
research.   He submitted this map to the Senate on the
6th of October, 1732, that is, two years and a half after
Bering's proposition to undertake the Great Northern

Expedition, but this did not deter him, in 1750, from ascribing to himself, on the basis of this same map and an accompanying memoir, Bering's proposition, nor from publishing an entirely perverted account of Bering's second expedition. He clung to all of his brother's conjectures about Gamaland, Kompagniland, and Staatenland as well as Jeço, although they were based on very unreliable accounts and the cartographical distortions of several generations. On the other hand, he most arbitrarily rejected all Russian accounts of far more recent and reliable origin, so that only Bering's and part of Yevrinoff's and Lushin's outlines of the first Kuriles were allowed to appear on the official map. He would rather reject all Russian works that could be made doubtful, than his brother's authority, and even in 1753, over twenty years after Spangberg's and Bering's voyages, he persistently sought to maintain his brother Guillaume's and his own unreasonable ideas concerning the cartography of this region. It was in part this dogged persistence in clinging to family prejudices that robbed Spangberg of his well-earned reward and brought Bering's last expedition to a sad end.

When the second Kamchatkan expedition left St. Petersburg, a copy of De l'Isle's map was given to Bering as well as to La Croyère. De l'Isle wrote the latter's instructions—ably written, by the way—and it was a result of his efforts that the Senate ordered Bering and Chirikoff to consult with La Croyère concerning the route to America,—a very reasonable decree in case he had been a good geographer. As it was, the order simply meant that they were to go according to the regulations

of De l'Isle in St. Petersburg. In the ship's council on
the 4th of May, 1741, La Croyère immediately produced
the above-mentioned map, and directed the expedition first
to find Gamaland, which, it was claimed, could lie but a
few days' sailing toward the southeast, and would furnish good assistance in finding America. But La Croyère
was only a spokesman for his brother, who in his memoir
had constructed his principal reasoning on this basis. He
says here that America can be reached from the Chukchee peninsula as well as from the mouth of the Kamchatka River, but with greatest ease and certainty from
Avacha Bay in a southeasterly direction to the northern
coast of Gamaland. In order to support this supposition
he adds: "It grieves me not to have found other information about this land seen by Don Juan de Gama than
what is given on the map of my late brother, his most
Christian Majesty's first geographer. But as he indicated
the position of this country with reference to Kompagniland and Jeço, and as I am certain, from other sources,
of the position of these two countries, I am consequently
convinced of their correct situation and distance from
Kamchatka."

That these miserable arguments exercised any influence upon the ship's council on the 4th of May, would
seem impossible, if we did not bear in mind the conduct
of the authorities in St. Petersburg. Two years previous
Spangberg had sailed right across Kompagniland, Staatenland and Jeço, and thus made every point in De l'Isle's
argument untenable. Bering and Chirikoff were familiar
with the results of these voyages, and shared Spangberg's
opinion. For this reason they could not possibly ascribe

any great importance to De l'Isle's directions which were
based on antiquated assumptions, but on the other hand,
they had neither moral nor practical independence enough
to take their own course.   The government laws, and
especially the Senate decrees, bound their hands.   They
were to submit all important measures to the action of
a commission, and were far from being sovereign com-
manders in any modern sense.   Under these circumstances they found it advisable, and possibly necessary, to
act in accordance with the opinion of these learned scholars, so as to be able later to defend themselves in every
particular against the criticisms of the Academy.   Hence
the commission resolved that the expedition should first
find the northern coast of Gamaland, follow this coast in
an easterly direction to America, and turn back in time to
be at home in Avacha Bay by the end of September.   In
this way their ships were carried far into the Pacific and
away from the Aleutian chain of islands, which, like the
thread of Ariadne, would speedily have led them to the
western continent.

CHAPTER XV.

THE DISCOVERY OF AMERICA FROM THE EAST.—STELLER
INDUCED TO JOIN THE EXPEDITION.—THE SEPARATION
OF THE ST. PETER AND THE ST. PAUL.

IN the course of the month of May the vessels were
equipped and supplied with provisions for five and
a half months, several cords of wood, 100 casks of water,
and two rowboats each. The St. Peter, commanded by
Bering, had a crew of 77, among whom were Lieutenant
Waxel, shipmaster Khitroff, the mates Hesselberg and
Jushin, the surgeon Betge, the conductor Plenisner,
Ofzyn (whom we remember as the officer who had been
reduced in rank), and Steller. On board the St. Paul,
commanded by Lieut. Alexei Chirikoff, were found the
marine officers Chegatchoff and Plautin, La Croyère, and
the assistant surgeon Lau,—in all about 76 men. Before
his departure, Bering had a very difficult matter to
arrange. His instructions directed him to take with him
to America a mineralogist; but when Spangberg had
started out on his unexpected expedition to Japan, Bering
had sent with him the mineralogist Hartelpol, and now
he found it impossible in East Siberia to get a man to fill
his place. Hence, as early as February, Bering applied to
Steller and tried to induce him to take upon himself the
duties of naturalist and mineralogist on this expedition.

Steller was born at Windsheim, Germany, in 1709. He first studied theology and had even begun to preach, when the study of science suddenly drew him from the church. He studied medicine and botany, passed the medical examinations in Berlin, and lectured on medicine in Halle. Then, partly as a matter of necessity and partly from a desire to travel, he went to Danzig, where he became surgeon on a Russian vessel, and finally, after a series of vicissitudes, he landed in St. Petersburg as a lecturer in the Academy of Science. According to his own desire he went to Siberia as Gmelin's and Müller's assistant, and, as these gentlemen found it altogether too uncomfortable to travel any farther east than Yakutsk, he took upon himself the exploration of Kamchatka. He was an enthusiast in science, who heeded neither obstacles nor dangers, a keen and successful observer, who has enriched science with several classical chapters, and had an ardent and passionate nature that attacked without regard to persons every form of injustice. His pen could be shaped to epigrammatic sharpness, and his tongue spared no one. In 1741, he wished to extend his investigations to Japan, and had, when Bering sought to secure his services, sent to the Academy a request to be permitted to participate in Spangberg's third expedition. Steller had, however, great hesitancy about leaving his special field of investigation without orders or permission, and Bering had to assume all responsibility to the Senate and Academy, and also secure for him from a council of all the ship's officers an assurance of the position as mineralogist of the expedition, before he could be induced to accept. Bering is said to have charged him verbally to make observations in all the departments of natural history, and promised him all necessary assistance. Steller accuses Bering of not having kept his promises, and, although he preserved until the last a high regard for Bering's seamanship and noble character, there nevertheless developed, during the expedition, a vehement enmity between Steller and the naval officers, especially Waxel and Khitroff, and this enmity found very pregnant expression in Steller's diary,* which, in this respect, is more a pamphlet than a description of travel. It is impossible, however, with our present resources, to ascertain the true state of affairs. Concerning Bering's voyage to America, we have only the St. Peter's journals kept by Waxel, Jushin, and Khitroff, and an account by Waxel, all of which have been used by Sokoloff in the preparation of the memoirs of the hydrographic department. Steller's diary, which goes into a detailed account of things in quite a different way than the official reports, was also used by Sokoloff, but as the latter had but little literary taste and still less sympathy for the contending parties, especially for Bering, he does not attempt to dispense justice between them. Steller's criticism must be looked upon as an eruption of that ill-humor which so often and so easily arises in the relations between the chief of an expedition and the accompanying scientists, between men with divergent interests and different aims. Bering and Steller, Cook and his naturalists, Kotzebue and Chamisso, are prominent examples of this disagreement. It is well known that Cook called the naturalists "the damned disturbers of the peace," and that he more than once threatened to put them off on

* Note 56.

some island or other in the ocean. Steller accuses Bering
of having too much regard for his subordinate officers,
but in all likelihood these had made the countercharge
that he gave too much heed to the scientists. At any
rate, Bering has often been blamed for—in accordance
with his instructions—letting La Croyère take part in the
councils at Avacha. But we must not forget that Steller
was a hot-headed and passionate fellow who persistently
maintained his own opinions. From many points in his
accounts, it appears that during this whole expedition he
was in a state of geographical confusion ; and even after
his return he seemed to imagine that the two continents
were separated by simply a narrow channel. He was
guided by observations of a scientific nature, and, as the
course of the St. Peter was no farther from the Aleutian
Islands than the appearance of seaweed, seals, and birds
indicated, he constantly imagined that they were off the
coast of the New World. The naval officers, on the other
hand, sought guidance in sounding ; but as their course
carried them out upon the great depths of the Pacific, the
northern wall of which very precipitously ascends to the
Aleutian Islands, their measurements were of no assistance, and in various points Steller was undoubtedly correct. The principal reason for Steller's complaint must
be sought in Bering's illness, and it is easily perceived
that, if the scurvy had not at a very early stage undermined his strength, his superior seamanship would have
secured the expedition quite different results than those
that were obtained.

    After a prayer service, the ships weighed anchor on the
4th of June, 1741. Expectations on board were great,—

the New World was to open up before them. According to the plan adopted, a southeasterly course was taken, and in spite of some unfortunate friction, Bering gave Chirikoff the lead, so as to leave him no cause for complaint. They kept their course until the afternoon of June 12, when they found themselves, after having sailed over six hundred miles in a southeasterly direction, in latitude 46° 9' N. and 14° 30' east of Avacha. According to De l'Isle's map they should long before have come to the coasts of Gamaland, but as they only saw sea and sky, Bering gave the command to turn back. With variable and unfavorable winds, they worked their way, during the few succeeding days, in a direction of N. N. E. up to latitude 49° 30', where Chirikoff, on the 20th of June, in storm and fog, left Bering and sailed E. N. E. in the direction of the American coast, without attempting to keep with the St. Peter. This was the first real misfortune of the expedition. For forty-eight hours Bering kept close to the place of separation, in hopes of again joining the St. Paul, and, as this proved fruitless, he convened a ship's council, at which it was decided to give up all further search for the St. Paul ; it was also resolved — in order to remove every doubt — to sail again to the 46th degree to find Gamaland. Having arrived here, some birds were seen, whereupon they continued their course to 45° 16' N. and 16° 23' east of Avacha, but of course without any results. During the four succeeding weeks, the ship's course was between north and east, toward the western continent, but as on their southern course they had come out upon the depths of Tuscarora, which, several thousand fathoms deep, run

right up to the Aleutian reef, their soundings gave them
no clue to land, although they were sailing almost parallel with this chain of islands. But Bering was now confined to his cabin. The troubles he had passed through,
his sixty years of age, and the incipient stages of scurvy,
had crushed his powers of resistance, while his officers,
Waxel and Khitroff, dismissed Steller's observations with
scornful sarcasm. Not until the 12th of July did they
take any precautions against a sudden landing. They
took in some of the sails during the night and hove to.
They had then been on the sea about six weeks. Their
supply of water was about half gone, and according to the
ship's calculations, which show an error of 8°, they had
sailed $46\frac{1}{2}°$ (*i. e.*, $54\frac{1}{2}°$) from the meridian of Avacha.
The ship's council therefore concluded, on the 13th of
July, to sail due north, heading N. N. E., and at noon
on the 16th of July, in a latitude by observation of
58° 14′ and a longitude of $49\frac{1}{2}°$ east of Avacha, they
finally saw land to the north.* The country was elevated, the coast was jagged, covered with snow, inhospitable, and girt with islands, behind which a snow-capped
mountain peak towered so high into the clouds that it
could be seen at a distance of seventy miles. "I do not
remember," says Steller, "of having seen a higher mountain in all Siberia and Kamchatka." This mountain

* H. H. Bancroft, History of Alaska, p. 79, has the following note: "The
date of Bering's discovery, or the day when land was first sighted by the
lookout, has been variously stated. Müller makes it the 20th of July, and
Steller the 18th; the 16th is in accordance with Bering's journal, and according to Bering's observation the latitude was 58° 28′. This date is confirmed
by a manuscript chart compiled by Petroff and Waxel, with the help of the
original log-books of both vessels. The claim set up by certain Spanish
writers in favor of Francisco Gali as first discoverer of this region is based
on a misprint in an early account of his voyage. For particulars see Hist.
Cal., I., this series."—TR.

was the volcano St. Elias, which is about 18,000 feet
high. *Bering had thus succeeded in discovering America
from the east.* As they had a head wind, they moved very
slowly toward the north, and not until the morning of the
20th did they cast anchor off the western coast of an
island which they called Sct. Ilii (St. Elias) in honor of
the patron saint of the day. On the same day, Khitroff
with fifteen men went, in the ship's boat, to search for a
harbor and to explore the island and its nearest surroundings. Steller, who had desired to accompany him, was
put ashore with the crew that brought fresh water from
St. Elias, and endeavored, as well as it was possible in a
few hours, to investigate the natural history of the island.
Khitroff circumnavigated the island and found various
traces of human habitation. Thus, on one of the adjacent
islands, a timbered house was found containing a fireplace,
a bark basket, a wooden spade, some mussel shells, and a
whetstone, which apparently had been used for sharpen-
ing copper implements. In an earth-hut another detach-
ment had found some smoked fish, a broken arrow, the
remains of a fire, and several other things. The coast of
the mainland, which was mountainous with snow-capped
peaks, was seen at a distance of eight miles. A good harbor was found on the north side of the large island. All
the islands were covered with trees, but these were so low
and slender that timber available for yards was not to be
found. On his venturesome wanderings here, only now
and then accompanied by a Cossack, Steller penetrated
these woods, where he discovered a cellar, which contained articles of food and various implements. As some
of these things were sent on board, Bering, by way of

indemnification, caused to be placed there an iron kettle, a pound of tobacco, a Chinese pipe, and a piece of silk cloth.

CHAPTER XVI.

BERING'S PLACE OF LANDING ON THE AMERICAN COAST. — CAPTAIN COOK'S UNCERTAINTY. — THE QUESTION DISCUSSED AND DEFINITELY SETTLED.

IN geographical literature complete uncertainty in regard to Bering's island St. Elias and its situation off the American coast still prevails. This uncertainty is due partly to Müller and partly to Cook. Müller is inaccurate; in fact, confused. He says that Bering saw the American continent in a latitude of 58° 28', and at a difference of longitude from Avacha of 50° (in reality, 58° 14' and 56° 30'), but he gives neither the latitude nor longitude of the island of St. Elias, which is the important point, and on his map of 1758, where he goes into details more than in his description, he marked on latitude 58° 28': "*Coast discovered by Bering in 1741.*" On such vague reports nothing can be based. In the ship's journal, however, which Müller in all likelihood must have seen, the latitude of the island is entered as 59° 40', and the longitude, according to the ship's calculations, as 48° 50' east of Avacha. But as Bering's calculations, on account of the strong current, which in these waters flows at a rate of twenty miles, had an error of about 8°, the longitude becomes 56° 30' east of Avacha, and at this astronomical point, approximately

correct, lies Kayak Island, which is Cook's Kayes Island,
having a latitude of 59° 47' and a longitude of 56° 44'
east of Avacha, and hence the question is to prove that
this island really is the Guanahani of the Russians, that
is, St. Elias.

Cook is the authority for the opinion which has
hitherto prevailed ; but surely no one can be more
uncertain and cautious on this point than he. He says:
" Müller's report of the voyage is so abbreviated, and his
map is so extremely inaccurate, that it is scarcely possible
from the one or the other, or by comparing both, to
point out a single place that this navigator either saw or
landed on. If I were to venture an opinion on Bering's
voyage along this coast, I should say that he sighted land
in the vicinity of Mt. Fairweather. But I am in no way
certain that the bay which I named in his honor is the
place where he anchored. Nor do I know whether the
mountain which I called Mt. St. Elias is the same
conspicuous peak to which he gave this name, and I am
entirely unable to locate his Cape St. Elias."

It would seem that such uncertain and reserved opinions were scarcely liable to be repeated without comment
or criticism. But nevertheless, the few reminiscences of
this chapter of Bering's explorations which our present
geography has preserved are obtained principally from
Cook's map ; for the first successors of this great
navigator, Dixon, 1785, La Pérouse, 1786, Malespina,
1791, and Vancouver, 1792, through whose efforts the
northwest coast was scientifically charted, maintained,
with a few unimportant changes, Cook's views on this
point. According to these views, Bering Bay was in

59° 18' north latitude and 139° west longitude, but Cook
had not himself explored this bay; he had simply found
indications of a bay, and hence La Pérouse and
Vancouver, whose explorations were much more in
detail, and who at this place could find no bay, were
obliged to seek elsewhere for it. La Pérouse puts Bering
Bay 10' farther south, at the present Alsekh River,
northwest of Mt. Fairweather, the lagoon-shaped mouth
of which he calls *Rivière de Bering,* and Vancouver was
of the opinion that in La Pérouse's *Bay de Monti,*
Dixon's Admiralty Bay, 59° 42' N. lat., he had found
Bering's place of landing. Vancouver's opinion has
hitherto held its own. The names Bering Bay, Admiralty Bay, or, as the Russians call it, Yakutat, are found
side by side; the latter, however, is beginning to displace
the former, and properly so, for Bering was never in or
near this bay.*

While this Cook cartography fixed Bering's place of
landing too far east, the Russians committed the opposite
error. On the chart with which the Admiralty provided
Captain Billings on his great Pacific expedition, the
southern point of the Island of Montague, in Prince
William's Sound, (the Russian name of the island is
Chukli), is given as Bering's promontory St. Elias, and
the Admiralty gave him the right, as soon as the
expedition reached this point, to assume a higher military
rank, something which he actually did. But Admiral
Krusenstern, with his usual keenness, comes as near the
truth as it was possible without having Bering's own
chart and the ship's journal. He thinks that, according

* Note 57.

to Steller's narrative, the St. Peter must have touched
America farther west than Yakutat Bay, and considers
it quite probable that their anchoring place must be
sought at one of the passages leading into Controller
Bay, either between Cape Suckling (which on Russian
maps is sometimes called Cape St. Elias) and Point
Le Mesurier, or between the islands Kayak and
Wingham. We shall soon see that this last supposition
is correct. O. Peschel has not ventured wholly to accept
Krusenstern's opinion, but he nevertheless calls attention
to the fact that Bering Bay is not correctly located. He
fixes Bering's landing place west of Kayak Island, and
contends against considering Mt. St. Elias as the
promontory seen by Bering, something which would
seem quite superfluous.*

This uncertainty is all the more striking, as, from
the beginning of this century, there have been accessible,
in the works of Sauer and Sarycheff, facts enough to
establish the identity of the island of St. Elias with the
present Kayak Island, and since the publication of
Bering's own map, in 1851, by the Russian Admiralty,
there can no longer be a shadow of a doubt. The map
is found in the appendix of this work, and hence a
comparison between the islands of St. Elias and Kayak
is possible (Map IV). The astronomical situation of the
islands, their position with reference to the mainland,
their surroundings, coast-lines, and geographical exten-
sion, the depths of the sea about both—everything proves
that they are identical; and, moreover, Sauer's and
Sarycheff's descriptions, which are quite independent of

* Note 58.

the St. Peter's journal, coincide exactly with the journal's references to the island of St. Elias. Sauer says that the island, from its most southerly point, extends in a north-easterly direction ("trend north 46° east"), that it is twelve English miles long and two and a half miles wide, that west of the island's most northerly point there is a smaller island (Wingham), with various islets nearer the mainland, by which a well-protected harbor is formed behind a bar, with about seven feet of water at ebb-tide, —hence just at the place where Khitroff, as we have already seen, found an available harbor for the St. Peter. The journal, as well as Steller, describes St. Elias as mountainous, especially in the southern part, thickly covered with low, coniferous trees, and Waxel particularly mentions the fact that off the coast of the island's southern point, Bering's Cape St. Elias, there was a single cliff in the sea, a "kekur," which is also marked on the map. Sarycheff and Sauer speak of Kayak Island as mountainous and heavily timbered. Its southern extremity rises above the rest of the island and ends very abruptly in a naked, white, saddle-shaped mountain. A solitary cliff of the same kind of rock, a pyramid-shaped pillar ("kekur," "*Abspringer*") lies a few yards from the point. Cook, too, in his fine outlines of Kayak Island, puts this cliff directly south of the point. If we then consider that the true dimensions of Bering's island plainly point to Kayak, that his course along the new coast is possible only on the same supposition that the direction in which Bering from his anchorage saw Mt. St. Elias exactly coincides with this mountain's position with reference to Kayak, that the soundings given by him

agree with those of Kayak, but do not agree with those
of Montague Island, which is surrounded by far more
considerable depths that have none of the above described
characteristics, and which, moreover, has so great a
circumference that Khitroff could not possibly have circumnavigated it in twelve hours, and finally, considering the fact that everything which Steller gives as
signs that a large current debouched near his anchorage finds an obvious explanation in the great Copper
or Atna estuary, in 60° 17' N., then it will be difficult to resist the conviction that *Kayak is Bering's
St. Elias, and that Vancouver's Cape Hammond is his
Cape St. Elias.*

Moreover, the traditions of the natives corroborate
this conclusion. While Billings's expedition was in Prince
William's Sound, says Sauer, an old man came on board
and related that every summer his tribe went on hunting
expeditions to Kayak.* Many years before, while he was
a boy, the first ship came to the island and anchored
close to its western coast. A boat was sent ashore, but
when it approached land all the natives fled, and not
until the ship had disappeared did they return to their
huts, where in their underground store-rooms they found
some beads, leaves (tobacco), an iron kettle, and some
other things. Sarycheff gives an account of this meeting, which in the main agrees with Billings's. These
stories also agree with Steller's account.†

These facts have not before, so far as the author
knows, been linked together, but Sokoloff states, without proof, however, that Bering's landfall was Kayak

Island.* This correct view is now beginning to find its way into American maps, where, in the latest works, Cape St. Elias will be found in the proper place, together with a Bering Haven on the northern coast of Kayak.†

*Bancroft, History of Alaska, p. 79, presents the same view: "The identity of Kayak is established by comparing Bering's with Cook's observations, which would be enough even if the chart appended to Khitroff's journal had not been preserved. At first both Cook and Vancouver thought it Yakutat Bay, which they named after Bering, but both changed their minds. As late as 1787 the Russian Admiralty college declared that the island Chukli (Montague of Vancouver) was the point of Bering's discovery, but Admiral Sarycheff, who examined the journals of the expedition, pointed at once to Kayak Island as the only point to which the description of Bering and Steller could apply. Sarycheff made one mistake in applying the name of Cape St. Elias to the nearest point of the mainland called Cape Suckling by Cook."—TR.

† Note 61.

CHAPTER XVII.

IT is by no means an easy matter to form an unbiased
opinion of Bering's stay off Kayak Island. Steller
is about our only authority, but just at the point where
it is most difficult to supplement his account, he gives
vent to most violent accusations against the management
of the expedition from a scientific standpoint. On the
16th of July, when land was first seen, he says: "One
can easily imagine how happy all were to see land. No
one failed to congratulate Bering, as chief of the expedition, to whom above all others the honor of discovery
belonged. Bering, however, heard all this, not only with
great indifference, but, looking toward land, he even
shrugged his shoulders in the presence of all on board."
Steller adds that on account of this conduct charges
might have been preferred against him in St. Petersburg,
had he lived.

As Bering during the first few succeeding days did not
make any preparations for a scientific exploration of the
country, as he even tried, according to Steller's assurance,
to dissuade the latter from making the island a visit, and

as Steller only through a series of oaths and threats (for thus p. 30 must undoubtedly be interpreted) could obtain permission to make, without help or even a guard for protection, a short stay on the island, his anger grew to rage, which reached its culmination on the following morning when Bering suddenly gave orders that the St. Peter should leave the island. "The only reason for this," he says, "was stupid obstinacy, fear of a handful of natives, and pusillanimous homesickness. For ten years Bering had equipped himself for this great enterprise; the explorations lasted ten hours !" Elsewhere he says derisively that they had gone to the New World "simply to bring American water to Asia."

These accusations must seem very serious to every modern reader. Unfortunately for Bering, his second voyage is of interest principally from the standpoint of natural history. It is especially naturalists that have studied it. They are predisposed to uphold Steller. Hence his account threatens wholly to undermine Bering's reputation, and as a matter of course, W. H. Dall, in discussing this subject, finds opportunity to heap abuse upon Bering. He says: "On the 18th of July, Bering saw land. On the 20th he anchored under an island. Between two capes, which he called St. Elias and St. Hermogenes, was a bay where two boats were sent for water and to reconnoitre. * * * With characteristic imbecility, Bering resolved to put to sea again on the next day, the 21st of July. Sailing to the northward, the commander was confused among the various islands, and sailed hither and thither, occasionally landing, but making no explorations, and showing his total incapacity for the position he occupied. He took to his bed, and Lieutenant Waxel assumed charge of the vessel." *

This is not writing history. It is only a series of errors and incivilities. It was *not* the 18th of July that Bering first saw land. He did *not* sail north from Kayak, but southwest, and hence could not have lost his course among islands, for here there are no islands. Nor did he sail hither and thither, but kept the course that had been laid out, and charted the coasts he saw in this course. The most ridiculous part of this is what this nautical author tells of the bay between Cape St. Elias and Cape St. Hermogenes (Marmot Island off the coast of Kadiak Island), for these points are farther apart than Copenhagen and Bremen. If, according to this writer, Bering was unpardonably stupid, he must have been, on the other hand, astonishingly "far-sighted." After these statements it will surprise no one that this author considers illness a kind of crime, and blames a patient, sixty years of age, suffering with the scurvy, for taking to his bed! If Mr. Dall had taken the trouble to study the Bering literature to which he himself refers in his bibliography of Alaska, he would have been in a position to pass an independent opinion of the navigator, and would certainly have escaped making this series of stupid statements. His words now simply serve to show how difficult it is to eradicate prejudice, and how tenacious of life a false or biased judgment can be. Death prevented Bering from defending and explaining his conduct. No one has since that time sought to render him justice. I therefore consider it my duty—even if

* Note 62.

I should seem to be yielding to the biographer's beset-
ting sin—to produce everything that can be said in
Bering's defense.

In the first place, then, it must be remembered that
on the 21st of July Bering had provisions left for no more
than three months, and that these were not good and
wholesome. His crew, and he himself, were already suffering from scurvy to such an extent that two weeks later
one-third of them were on the sick-list. Furthermore,
he was over fifty-six degrees of longitude from his nearest
port of refuge, with a crew but little accustomed to the
sea. The American coast in that latitude was not,
according to Bering's judgment, nor is it according to our
present knowledge, in any way a fit place to winter, and
besides, he knew neither the sea nor its islands and depths,
its currents and prevailing winds. All this could not but
urge him to make no delay. And, in fact, Steller himself
expressly says that it was a series of such considerations
that determined Bering's conduct. "Pusillanimous
homesickness" can scarcely have had any influence on
a man who from his youth had roamed about in the
world and lived half a generation in the wilds of Siberia. "The good Commander," thus Steller expresses himself, "was far superior to all the other officers in divin-
ing the future, and in the cabin he once said to myself
and Mr. Plenisner: 'We think now that we have found
everything, and many are pregnant with great expectations; but they do not consider where we have landed,
how far we are from home, and what yet may befall us.
Who knows but what we may meet trade winds that
will prevent our return? We are unacquainted with the

country, and are unprovided with provisions for wintering here.'"

It must be conceded that his position was one fraught
with difficulties. At this point there are two things which
Steller either has not correctly understood, or suppresses.
According to his instructions, Bering was authorized to
spend two years and make two voyages in the discovery
of America, and to undertake another expedition afterwards with new preparations and equipments. And in his
explanations to the crew he calls special attention to this
point. Under these circumstances it would not have been
right in him to assume any more risks than absolutely
necessary. But here again the old opposition between
Bering's nautico-geographical and Steller's physico-geographical interests breaks out. As a discoverer of the old
school Bering's principal object was to determine some
elementary geographical facts : namely, the distribution
of land and water along the new coast, and hence he left
Kayak Island, not to reach Avacha as soon as possible,
but to follow the coast of the newly discovered country
toward the west and north. All authorities agree on this
point. It was illness and the Aliaska peninsula, projecting so far into the ocean as it does, that prevented him
from sailing up toward latitude 65°, his real goal. Even
Steller testifies to this, and although he repeats his former
accusations against Bering, it does not signify anything,
as he was excluded from the councils and was obliged to
guess at what was adopted. His accusations are especially
insignificant from the fact that he definitely contradicts
himself on this point, for later on in his narrative he says
that not until the 11th of August was it resolved, on

account of the approaching autumn and the great distance from home, to start immediately on the return voyage to Kamchatka. That is to say, they had not then made a start. Until the 11th of August, for three weeks after their departure from Kayak, Bering pursued his task of nautical discovery along the new coast, and it would seem that he can be blamed for nothing more than considering this work of the expedition more important than that of the physico-geographical investigation which Steller represented. This was but natural. It was merely accidental that Steller accompanied Bering, and through him the expedition received a modern cast, which was not at all designed, and which Bering desired to make use of only under favorable circumstances. We may regret his haste, and we may especially regret the fact that so keen and clever a naturalist as Steller did not get an opportunity to explore the regions west of Mount St. Elias before European trade and white adventurers put in an appearance ; but it hardly seems a question of doubt whether anyone for that reason has a right to make accusations against the chief of the expedition.

It was very early on the morning of July 21 that the chief suddenly, and contrary to his custom, appeared on deck and gave the command to weigh anchor and stand out to sea. In doing this he set aside his instructions from headquarters to act in accordance with the ship's council. He acted as a sovereign chief, and notwithstanding the fact that both of his lieutenants thought it wrong to leave the newly discovered coast without an adequate supply of water, he overruled all objections and informed them that he assumed all responsibility for

his conduct. He was convinced of the entire necessity
of it, he said, and thought it unsafe to remain longer in
this exposed anchorage. Time did not permit him to go
in search of the harbor found by Khitroff on the day
previous, and there was moreover a seaward breeze. One
fourth of the water-casks remained unfilled.

Before a strong east wind, the St. Peter on that day
made fifty miles on a southwesterly course. During
the two succeeding days, he continued in this general
direction. It was misty, and the coast was invisible, but
the sounding-line continued to show a depth of from
forty to fifty fathoms. In a council, concerning the
deliberations of which Steller has a very confused and
incorrect account, it was decided, on July 25, to sail
slowly towards Petropavlovsk and, at intervals as wind
and weather permitted, to head for the north and west, in
order to explore the coast they had left.

They continued on their southwesterly course, and on
the next morning, July 26, they were off the Kadiak
archipelago. In a latitude of 56° 30', and about sixteen
miles toward the north, they saw a high and projecting
point, which Bering called St. Hermogenes, in honor of
the patron saint of the day. He thought that this point
was a continuation of the continent they had left behind
them, and as such it is represented on both Müller's and
Krasilnikoff's manuscript maps in the archives of the
Admiralty. On his third voyage, Cook explored the
Kadiak group, which he too had assumed to be a part of
the mainland. He now found that Bering's promontory
was a small island east of Afognak, but out of respect for
Bering, he retained the original name. Krusenstern also

calls it St. Hermogenes Island, but later the Russians changed it to Euratchey Island, on account of the great number of marmots there, and since the United States came into possession of it, the name has been translated, and it is now known as Marmot Island.* Steller has not a single word in his diary about St. Hermogenes, and besides, his account at this point is full of inaccuracies.

"Consequently, until July 26," he says, "we sailed along the coast, as these gentlemen thought it was necessary to follow it, while it would have been sufficient, at intervals of a hundred versts, to have sailed a degree or two toward the north." He thus blames them for not having followed the method which at about that time they had agreed upon, and later did follow. His story of their having, for the first five days, sailed along the coast, simply proves, in connection with a series of other incidents in his work, that things were not entered in his diary daily, but written down later from memory; hence its value as proof is considerably diminished.

Along the southeastern coast of Kadiak the voyage was very dangerous. The average depth was twenty-five fathoms; the water was very roily, the weather heavy with fog and rain, and the wind violent. Not until the 31st of July was the weather clear enough for an observation, when they found themselves in a latitude of 54° 49', and had passed the Kadiak archipelago.

In accordance with the plan adopted, they here veered to the northwest to seek the mainland for the purpose of determining its trend. On the night of August 1 (and 2), they suddenly approached land, having only four fathoms

* Note 63.

of water below the keel. There was a heavy fog, no wind,
and a swift current, but they succeeded in shifting about
and getting out into eighteen fathoms of water, where
they anchored to await daybreak. In the morning, at
eight o'clock, a small island was seen at a distance of four
miles. It was three miles long, with an east to west
trend. A long reef extended out into the sea from the
eastern point, seen by them in a direction E. S. E. by E.
In the evening they weighed anchor, having a heavy fog,
and on the next morning, the island was seen at a distance of seven geographical miles toward the south. Its
latitude was calculated as 55° 32', but as all of Bering's
determinations of latitude on his return voyage from
America show an error of from 30' to 45' less than the
true latitude, it must be concluded that the island was
in latitude 56° and some minutes. He called the island
St. Stephen from the calendar day, but his crew or
lieutenants must have called it Foggy Island (Tumannoi),
as even Krasilnikoff's manuscript map, in the possession
of the Admiralty, has this name. Later the cartography
of this region became considerably confused. The name
St. Stephen disappeared. Cook called another island Fog
Island, while it became customary to consider the island
discovered by Bering as identical with Ukamok (Chirikoff Island, Vancouver's Island), where the Russians had
a colony, and thus the island itself was finally lost to
geography. Notwithstanding the fact that Admiral
Krusenstern, in a clever essay, has given an able
review of the literature pertaining to this question,
and has shown that where Bering saw St. Stephen,
Cook, Sarycheff, and Vancouver likewise saw an island,

different from Ukamok, and regardless of the fact that for these reasons he restored St. Stephen on his map, Lieutenant Sokoloff, who most recently, in Russian literature, has treated Bering's voyage to America, has wholly disregarded Krusenstern's essay, and says that St. Stephen is identical with Ukamok. Sokoloff's essay is very superficial, and, compared with Krusenstern's weighty reasons, is based on mere supposition. But, although the map of the North Pacific, in the Russian Admiralty (1844), has a Tumannoi Island (that is, Foggy Island, St. Stephen) somewhat northeast of Ukamok, it must be admitted that, until the United States undertakes a new and careful survey of the Aliaska peninsula and its southern surroundings, this question can not be thoroughly decided, probable as it may be that Bering and Krusenstern are both right.

August 3, the voyage was continued toward the northwest. In a latitude of 56° (according to Steller) they saw the high snow-capped mountain peaks of the Aliaska peninsula in a direction N. N. W. by W., but on account of stormy and foggy weather they sought, with an easterly wind, to get back into their main course. Thus they reached, August 4, the Jefdokjejefski Islands in a direction S. S. E. ¾ by E., at a distance of twenty miles from 55° 45' N. These form a group of seven high and rocky islands, which on Russian maps still bears the same name, but in West Europe this name has been displaced, and they are usually called the Semidi, or Semidin, Islands, the name of the largest of the group.

On August 7, they found themselves south of the Jefdokjejefski Islands. But now misfortunes began to

pour in upon them. They encountered adverse winds
which continued with but few interruptions during the
succeeding months. The St. Peter was tossed about on
the turbulent and unfamiliar waters of the Aleutian archipelago, where the crew experienced an adventure so
fraught with suffering and dire events that it is quite
beyond compare in the history of discoveries. At the
same time, the scurvy got the upper hand. Bering had
a severe attack which rendered him unfit for service.
With his illness the bonds of discipline were relaxed.
Under these circumstances there was called, on the 10th
of August, an extraordinary council, in which all the
officers participated. At this meeting it was finally
decided to give up the charting of the American coast,
and immediately start out upon the direct route home-
ward on parallel 52°, the latitude of Avacha. The
whole crew, from the highest to the lowest, signed this
resolution. The facts taken into consideration were that
September had been fixed as the extreme limit of time
within which to return home, and that they were then
in the middle of August. Avacha was at least 1600
miles distant, autumn was at hand with dark nights
and stormy weather, and sixteen of the crew were
already sick with the scurvy.

With a strong head-wind, in raw and foggy weather,
and now and then overtaken by fierce storms, they
worked their way slowly along until the 27th of August.
The condition of affairs on board had grown continually
worse, when it was finally announced that through carelessness and irregularity the supply of water had been
reduced to twenty-five casks, a quantity that could not

possibly suffice for the 1200 miles which, according to
their calculations, yet remained.   Hence it was necessary
once more to find land to take in water, and on the
27th the St. Peter's prow was again headed for Aliaska.
They sailed north one degree and a half, and after a
lapse of three days they reached a multitude of high
islands, behind which the coast of the mainland arose
in the distance.

August 30, the St. Peter lay at anchor off the Shumagins, a group of thirteen treeless, barren, and rocky
islands near the coast of Aliaska.   The journal gives their
situation as latitude 54° 48′ N. and longitude 35° 30′ E.
from Avacha.   While the latitude as here determined
has the usual error, referred to several times before,
the longitude has an error of 6½°.   Among these islands
the first death on board occurred.   It was the sailor
Shumagin, who, on the 30th, died in the hands of his
mates as they were taking him ashore.   The islands
were named in honor of him.   On the whole the situation was most deplorable.   Bering had fallen away so
much in his illness that he could not stand, and the
others that were sick were carried ashore, and lay scattered along the coast, giving this a very sad and sorrowful aspect.   Confusion and uncertainty grew apace, as
those in command could not maintain their authority.
Waxel and Khitroff, the highest in command, bandied
words, whereas the situation demanded firmness and
vigor.   The only one that preserved any manner of self-
possession and forethought was Steller.   He immediately went ashore, examined the vegetation of the island,
and collected a large number of anti-scorbutic plants,

especially scurvy-grass and berries, with which, in the
course of a week, he succeeded in restoring Bering to
sufficient strength to be able to use his limbs. Through
the use of the same remedies the other sufferers were
relieved. But Steller thought also of the future. The
medicine chest contained "plasters and salves for half
an army," but only extremely few real medicines, and
hence he suggested to Lieut. Waxel, who was then in
command, that he send a number of sailors ashore to
gather anti-scorbutic plants, but this excellent and
timely advice was rejected.

Furthermore, Steller used all his influence to procure
good water. He went ashore with the sailors for this
purpose, and as they began to dip water from the first
pool they found, one, too, which was connected with
the sea during high tide, he directed them to fresh
springs a little farther in the interior, but the crew sent
some samples on board, and from there came the report
that the water was good enough. Thus it was that a
new cause of disease—in spite of Steller's protestations—
was added to all the others. The water was brackish,
and on standing in the casks became unfit for use.

On the whole the stay at the Shumagins, which was
unnecessarily prolonged, was very unfortunate. The St.
Peter lay at anchor south of them in a very exposed position. On the evening of August 29, a fire was seen on
one of the islands, and on this account, Khitroff wished
to explore them more thoroughly, although Waxel firmly
opposed releasing both of the ship's boats under the
present dangerous circumstances. By applying to Bering,
who was in the cabin, and hardly understood the situation,

Khitroff had his way, and left the ship with the yawl and five men. He was gone four days, during which time the St. Peter was forced to lie at anchor, while a favorable east wind might have carried them several hundred miles toward home. The yawl was dashed to pieces off one of the neighboring islands, and no more came from the expedition than that Lieutenant Waxel, under great difficulty, found it necessary to rescue the six shipwrecked adventurers. Moreover, they experienced a somewhat uninteresting clash with the Innuit (Esquimo)* inhabitants of the Aliaska peninsula, of which Müller and Steller both give a detailed account.

* For a full description of these people see H. H. Bancroft, Native Races, Vol. I.—TR.

CHAPTER XVIII.

THE St. Peter left the Shumagin Islands September 6,
and sailed southward to resume the direct course.
The weather was very bad, with alternating fogs, mist, and
storms. A west wind prevailed almost continuously.
Now and then a regular hurricane crossed their course.
If occasionally they had a favorable breeze, it seemed to
last but a few hours. "I know no harder, more fatiguing
life," says one of the St. Peter's officers, "than to sail
an unknown sea. I speak from experience, and with
truth can say that during the five months I spent on this
voyage, without seeing any place of which the latitude
and longitude had been fixed, I did not have many hours
of quiet sleep. We were in constant danger and uncertainty."

As a last resort, they even thought of returning to
America, or of reaching Japan. For several days they
were swept along by a storm. September 23, the second
death occurred, and on the 24th they again saw, to their
great astonishment, land toward the north. They were

then on about the 51st parallel. They were of the opinion
that they were fourteen degrees from the Shumagins, and
supposed that they were 21° 39' from Avacha, which of
course was very erroneous, for they were in the vicinity
of the present Atka. As they saw behind the islands a
high, snow-capped mountain, which, from the calendar
day, they called St. Johannes, they supposed the land to
be a continuation of the American continent.

During the next seventeen days, from the 25th of
September until the 11th of October, they carried their
lower sails only, and were driven by a stormy west wind
five degrees toward the southeast to a latitude of 48°.
"The wind," says Steller, "seemed as if it issued forth
from a flue, with such a whistling, roaring and rumbling,
that we expected every moment to lose mast and rudder,
or to see the ship crushed between the breakers. The
dashing of a heavy sea against the vessel sounded like
the report of a cannon, and even the old, experienced
mate, Andreas Hesselberg, assured us that during a
sailor's life of fifty years he had not before seen such a
sea." No one was able to stand at his post. The ship
was at the mercy of the angry elements. Half of the
crew were sick and feeble, the other half well from dire
necessity, but were confused and distracted by the great
danger. For many days no cooking could be done, and
all they had that was fit to eat was some burned ship-
biscuits, and even these were on the point of becoming
exhausted. No one showed any firmness of purpose;
their courage was as "unsteady as their teeth." The
officers now and then thought of returning to America,
but their plans changed as often as the weather.

During the first week in October it became very cold;
heavy storms of hail and snow swept over the ship and
made the work on board almost unendurable. On the
6th the ship's supply of brandy gave out, and, as the
storm from the southwest still continued to rage, Waxel
seriously proposed to return to America and seek a harbor
of refuge, as it would be necessary in a few days, on
account of the number on the sick list, to resign the ship
to the mercy of the waves.

Bering, however, refused to entertain this idea, and
exhorted the crew to make an offering to the church—
the Russians to the church in Petropavlovsk, the Luther-
ans to the church in Viborg, Finland, where Bering had
formerly resided.

As elsewhere on this whole voyage, Steller was here
geographically confused, and imagined that they were
sailing in a latitude of 50–53°, while in reality they were
on the 48th parallel, and hence his complaint that the
officers would not sail to this parallel to get a better
breeze, signifies nothing. Müller gives the correct position of the ship when he says that on the 12th of October
it was in latitude 48° 18', but he too is wrong when he
states that the weather did not permit them to make an
observation, for just at this time they had fair weather
and sunshine, and on the 11th, at noon, determined the
latitude as 48° 15' and the longitude as 27° east of
Avacha. During the succeeding ten days the weather
was somewhat more favorable. Clear weather, with heavy
frosts, prevailed; some hail and snow fell, but nevertheless they succeeded in making ten degrees on the
parallel of 49° 30'. The condition on board was getting

much worse. Poor water, lack of bread and spirits, the cold and wet, vermin and anxiety, undermined the last remnants of their powers of resistance. On the 19th the grenadier Kisseloff, on the 20th the servant Charitonoff, and on the 21st the soldier Luka Savjaloff, died. Even men apparently well were unable to stand at their posts from sheer want and exhaustion.

Then the water supply threatened to give out. They had but fifteen casks of water, a part of which was very poor. Waxel was again thinking of searching for land toward the north, when a strong wind carried them so far westward that they supposed they had passed all traces of American regions. They then determined to keep their course on the 52° of latitude, but on the following day, to their great astonishment, they sighted the Aleutian Islands and made some new discoveries. On October 25, at a distance of 8½ geographical miles toward the northwest, they saw a high, snow-capped island, which they called St. Marcus. By an observation at noon its latitude was found to be 50° 50', but as this island is our Amchitka, and as its southern extremity, according to Admiral Sarycheff, is in a latitude of 51° 35', it is evident that the St. Peter's determinations of latitude were constantly from one-half to three-fourths of a degree less than the true latitude. Later this fact had an extremely unfortunate effect on their resolutions. On October 28, Kiska, which Bering called St. Stephen, was discovered, besides three (in reality four) smaller islands east of it, and, carried along toward the north by a southwesterly wind, they sighted, on the morning of the 29th, some low islands, which are supposed to have been the present Semichi

Islands, situated east of Attu. These islands, which to
them appeared as one, were called St. Abraham Island.
According to the ship's journal they were seen at ten
o'clock in the morning at a distance of six miles toward
the west, and at noon ten miles in a direction W. S. W.
It is evident that the St. Peter sailed north of these islands, but as the latitude on that day was determined as
52° 31', at least 45' too far south, and as the ship undoubtedly on the 29th and 30th of October passed the Blizhni
group (the Nearer Aleutians) it is more than probable
that the strait between the most westerly of the Semichi
Islands and Attu was seen from the ship's deck, although
the officers do not mention this island in the journal, but
simply indicate it on the chart. It is, however, referred
to by both Müller and Steller. The most westerly of the
Semichi Islands and Attu must be the former's Deception
Islands. Steller applies all of his acuteness of mind to
show that they were the first two Kuriles. Nothing shows
better than this assertion how confused Steller was;
hence his unsparing attacks on Waxel, and his base
insinuations, are not of the least moment. "Betrayed
and sold by two unscrupulous leaders," he says, "we
sailed, after October 31, in a northerly direction from the
51st to the 56th parallel!" How unreasonable! They
were, already on the 30th, north of the 53d parallel. A
sharp southwest wind was blowing, several deaths were
occurring daily, the helmsmen were conducted to the
wheel by companions so deathly sick that they could
scarcely walk, the ship's rigging and sails were fast giving
way, the weather was raw and damp, the nights dark and
long, and all attempts at the determination of latitude

and longitude had about ceased. Under these circumstances was it not worthy of all honor that Waxel was still able to hold the vessel up to the wind at all and approach the Commander Islands from Attu ? In a short time the wind veered to the east, and on November 4 (Steller has it the 5th), in a latitude calculated at 53° 30', they saw an elevated coast in the west at a distance of about sixteen miles. It is impossible to describe the joy occasioned by this sight. The sick and half-dead crawled on deck to see land once more, and all thanked God for their merciful rescue. Bering, almost completely exhausted, was greatly revived, and all thought of how they would rest and restore their health and vigor. Hidden brandy casks were brought out, in order that by the Vodka's assistance they might properly celebrate the happy return. And in the first moments of their exultation even the officers rejoiced to think that their calculations were not entirely wrong.

All were agreed that they were off the mouth of Avacha Bay, and in the precipitous mountain sides of Copper Island they eagerly sought for the promontories which mark the entrance to that bay. The channel between Copper Island and Bering Island was hidden to their view, hence they thought they had reached Kamchatka. When, a little later, they saw through the mist the most northerly part of the strait, they were for a short time not indisposed to believe that they were near their home harbor. But soon an intense feeling of doubt seized them. According to the ship's reckoning, they were yet forty miles from Avacha. An observation at noon informed them they were at least one degree farther north than this place, and before evening came on, the coast-lines assumed an appearance that compelled them to give up all thought of having reached home. But, as Bering on his first voyage had not found land for several days' sailing east of the mouth of the Kamchatka River, they still clung to the belief that they were off the coast of the mainland. During the night, they stood to the north so as to steer clear of land, as they feared a storm. With great difficulty the topsails were taken in, but the feeble crew were obliged to leave the other sails. In the night a storm from the east rent the starboard shrouds of the mainmast so that it could no longer carry sail. The next morning, a bright and magnificent November day, the whole crew assembled for a final consultation.

All that could walk or crawl, officers as well as crew, dragged themselves into the chief's cabin to hear the result. I have repeatedly called attention to the fact that Bering did not have the sovereign power with which the chief of an expedition is now-a-days endowed. The terrible disease that had overpowered him still further lessened his influence; but never had the rules and regulations appeared in worse light than on this occasion. Waxel and Khitroff, who had resolved to make a landing, sought both before and during the meeting to induce the crew to vote for this resolution; but Bering opposed it and put forth the last remnants of his strength and energy to rescue the expedition. "We have still the foremast," he said, "and six casks of water. After having endured so much suffering and hardship, we must risk everything in order to reach Avacha." Waxel and

Khitroff immediately endeavored to counteract the influence of this good advice, but the subordinates were in
doubt, and would not sign any resolution except on the condition that the officers expressly assured them of the fact
that the adjacent coast was Kamchatka. This Khitroff
finally took upon himself to do, and so partly through
compulsion and partly through persuasion the lieutenants
succeeded in securing a majority for their proposition.
But even yet Bering sought to save his convictions, and
appealed to the reduced Lieutenant Ofzyn, who had had
charge of the explorations from the Obi to the Yenesei
and was now serving as a sailor on board the St. Peter;
but as he immediately expressed his agreement with
Bering, he was in most abusive language driven from
the cabin. Under these circumstances Steller found it
useless to support Bering. He confined himself to cer-
tifying to the very great enervation of the crew. Before
the council adjourned, it was resolved to make for the
coast, where the lieutenants, in an open bay, expected to
find a harbor.

Before an easy northeast breeze, the St. Peter drifted
toward the coast, without helmsman or commander. The
chief lay at death's door in his cabin, Waxel and Khitroff
were seeking rest and quiet, and not until the ship lay
about four miles from land did Steller induce Bering to
order them on deck. They soon began to sound, and
one verst from shore they cast anchor. Night came on
with bright moonlight. The ebb-tide receded over the
rocky beach, producing heavy breakers. In these the
ship was tossed about like a ball, until finally the cable
snapped. They now expected to be dashed against the

rocks at any moment. The confusion became indescrib-
able. In order not to have a corpse on board, the dead
bodies of two of their companions were thrown over-
board. It had been the intention to take them ashore for
burial. At this juncture the second anchor was lost;
but at the last moment, just as the third was on the
point of being cast, Ofzyn succeeded in establishing order
and keeping the anchor on board. The vessel glided
safely across the reefs, and in a few moments the boat-
swain and Ofzyn were able to anchor in a sheltered place.
The St. Peter was safe for the time being. In this still
and bright November night (the night of Nov. 6, 1741)
the ship was riding at anchor off the center of the northeast coast of Bering Island, scarcely 600 yards from
shore. Thus ended this frightful adventure. Very
fortunately, the ship had happened to strike the only
navigable channel on the east that leads to the coast of
the island.

It yet remains to determine with more exactness the
place of stranding. On this point literature offers no
reliable information. I am aware that Steller says that
the vessel stranded on the northern coast of the island,
but this is not to be taken literally. After the St. Peter
had passed the northern point of Copper Island, which
lies parallel with the trend of Bering Island, it was carried west and southwest by a northeasterly wind, and
hence would strike the coast of Bering Island off, or a
few minutes north of, the northern extremity of Copper
Island. At this point the eastern coast of Bering Island
recedes to the west and forms that bay which the officers
saw ahead. From this it is evident that the place where

the vessel ran ashore was four or five miles north of the present Cape Khitroff. In Waxel's journal the geographical position is entered as 55° 5' north latitude, but Fr. Lütke gives it as latitude 54° 58' and longitude 193° 23' west from Greenwich. On his large map of a part of the Aleutian Islands, with Russian and French text, he marks the place of landing at this point with these words: *" C'est près de cet endroit que le commandeur Bering a fait naufrage "** (*i. e.*, in the vicinity of this place Bering stranded). This place is at about the center of the eastern coast of the island, which extends at least 28' farther north to Cape Waxel, and hence only from a local point of view, just as it must have seemed to Steller as the vessel approached land, can this receding part of the coast be designated as the northern side of the island. The view here set forth is further corroborated by many places in Steller's diary, and by other accounts of the stay on the island.†

* Map III., Appendix.

† My view has been most strongly confirmed by the excellent Norwegian naturalist, Dr. Leonhard Stejneger, of the Smithsonian Institution, Washington, who in the years 1882-'84 passed eighteen months on Bering Island and circumnavigated it. In *Deutsche Geographische Blätter*, 1885, he describes his trip and gives a good contour map of the island, as well as of Bering's stranding-place, which in honor of him is still called " Komandor," and is situated in the place described above, on the northeastern coast of the island.—*Author's Note to American Edition.*

For Dr. Stejneger's final remarks on this point the reader is referred to Note 64, in the Appendix, where will be found a letter to the translator.

CHAPTER XIX.

THE island upon whose shores Bering, after a voyage
of four months, was cast, was a high, rocky, and
uninviting country. The snowless mountains of Plu-
tonic rock, wild and jagged, arose perpendicularly out
of the sea, and deep ravines with seething mountain
streams led into the treeless interior.* There was snow
on only the highest peaks, and on this cold November
night the coast appeared to the shipwrecked unfortu-
nates in all its naked and gloomy solitude, and hence

* Dr. Stejneger, to whom the translator is indebted for various notes
and corrections of scientific interest, says: "The mountains which Steller
and his companions saw were not eruptive rocks. The whole island consists of a more or less coarsely grained sandstone or conglomerate,— Plu-
tonic rock cropping out only in isolated spots. The mountain streams of
Bering Island are anything but 'seething'; on the contrary, they are as a
rule very quiet."

174

great was their surprise on landing to find the island
teeming with animal life, yet undisturbed by human
habitation. The Commander Islands, as the group is
now called, consist of two large islands and a few rocky
islets. The most easterly of the former is Copper Island
(Mednie), about thirty-five miles long and three miles
wide, covered with high, steep, and jagged mountains,
which lie athwart the main trend of the island, S. E.
to N. W., and terminate precipitously, often perpendicularly, with a narrow strand at the base scarcely
fifty feet wide. On a somewhat larger scale, the same
description applies to Bering Island, which, according
to Steller, is $23\frac{1}{2}$ geographical miles long and nearly $3\frac{1}{4}$
wide. It is situated about 30 geographical miles from
Kamchatka, between latitude 54° 40' and 55° 25' north,
and longitude 165° 40' and 166° 40' east of Greenwich.
Only on the west coast, within the shelter of the Sea
Lion Island (Arii Kamen) and a lesser islet, is there a
fairly good harbor, where the Russians later founded
the only colony of the island, consisting of a few Aleuts
who cultivate some vegetables, but maintain themselves
principally by hunting and fishing. For this purpose
they have built, here and there on the east coast, some
earth-huts which are used only temporarily. The very
high mountains, having a trend from N. W. to S. E., almost
everywhere extend clear to the sea, and only here and
there along the mouths of the brooks do semicircular
coves recede from 700 to 1300 yards into the interior.
In Bering's day these coves or rookeries contained a
fauna entirely unmolested by human greed and love of
chase, developed according to nature's own laws, for

which reason great scientific interest attaches to the
stranding of the St. Peter. Of this animal life Steller
gives us in his various works descriptions which are unex-
celled in power and fidelity. These have made Bering's
second voyage immortal. Naturalists will again and again
turn to them. For this reason it would seem that Steller
had no ground for complaint that Bering had taken him
from his real field of investigation : Kamchatka—a complaint made in our day by O. Peschel—for on Bering
Island he first found that field of labor and that material,
the description of which has immortalized his name.*

With the exception of the Arctic fox, the higher
fauna of these islands were found exclusively among

* Dr. Stejneger, ever on the alert to honor Steller, says in *Deutsche Geographische Blätter*, 1885: "It was due to Steller that not only a majority of
the participants survived, but that the expedition won a lasting name in
the history of science. Bering left his name to the island upon which he
died, and the group to which it belongs, Komandorski (Commander Islands),
was named after his rank. Moreover, Bering Sea, Bering Strait, a peninsula
in Asia, and a bay in America have been named in honor of him. But what
is there in these regions to remind one of the immortal Steller, the Herod-
otus of these distant lands ? Search the map of the island of which he has
given such a spirited description. His name is nowhere to be found, while
three capes have received the names of Bering's lieutenants and helmsmen,
who were the authors of the whole misfortune: Waxel, Khitroff, and Jushin.
The man that rescued and immortalized the expedition has fallen into
oblivion. I consider it an honor that it has been granted to me to render
long deferred justice to this great German investigator. The highest mountain peak on Bering's Island will henceforth be called Mount Steller."

In speaking of a description by Steller of some rock formations on the
western coast that resembled ancient ruins, Dr. S. says in the same article:
"I landed at the only remaining one of these arches, under which Steller
had probably walked. It is a fine specimen of a natural triumphal arch,
standing quite by itself. In honor of Steller I called it Steller's Triumphal
Arch. No monument marks his resting-place on the desert steppes of Siberia; Russia has never forgiven him for his ingenuous criticism of the injustice of her courts; but Steller's name will nevertheless live. His Triumphal
Arch, gaily decked with the variegated lichens *Caloplaca murorum* and
crenulata, and adorned with the lovely white golden-eyed blossoms of the
Chrysanthemum arcticum, is a monument that does fitting honor to the great
naturalist."—Tr.

STELLER'S TRIUMPHAL ARCH.

the sea mammals. The most important furred animal
at that time was the sea-otter (*Enhydra lutris*, Linn.),
which lived in families on the coast during the whole
year, especially, however, in the winter. Its velvety fur
brought about 100 rubles on the Chinese border, and
hence this animal later became the object of a most eager
search. Nordenskjöld says these otters have been driven
away, not only from Bering Island, but also from other
grounds, where formerly they were slaughtered by the
thousand. This statement, however, is not entirely correct. The sea-otter may still be found on Bering Island,

and on the adjacent Copper Island (Mednie) it is frequently found, and is protected by just such laws as Nordenskjöld demands for its preservation.

The greatest number of marine animals here were
found to belong to the family of eared seals (*Otariidæ*) ;
namely, the sea-lion (*Eumetopias Stelleri*), from which
oil is obtained, and the fur-seal (*Callorhinus ursinus*),
which is still the world's most important fur-bearing animal. Since the close of the last century, the Russian government has with great care sought to protect this animal,
and has built up a national enterprise which yields a large
annual income, and which makes it possible for the Russo-
American company which has a lease of the business, to
kill annually about 30,000 seals and still increase the stock.
On this point, too, Nordenskjöld's statements are unreliable and misleading. He puts the annual catch much too
high, which, at the time, caused no slight trouble between
the Russian government and the company.*

On the whole, it seems humiliating to West Europe
that it is only decried and tyrannical Russia that has
understood how to protect this useful animal. When
Russian America, the present Alaska, in 1867 was sold
to the United States, some of the best seal fisheries, the
Pribyloff Islands, were a part of the purchase. The
United States has found it profitable to retain the Russian regulations for seal hunting, for those small islands
alone yield the interest on the sum paid for the whole
territory.

* Dr. Stejneger, in "Contributions to the History of the Commander
Islands," published in Proceedings of U. S. Nat. Museum, 1882, p. 86, calls
attention to Professor Nordenskjöld's erroneous statement, and gives the
exact figures.—TR.

The eared seals put in their appearance on the Commander Islands in the spring, and are found in the rookeries by the hundreds of thousands until August or September. They proved of the greatest importance for the support of the shipwrecked expedition, and after the sea-otter for a circuit of many miles had been driven away, they furnished a part of the crew's daily means of sustenance.

But the most interesting animal on Bering Island was the sea-cow (*Rhytina Stelleri*),* a very large and ponderous animal from eight to ten meters long and weighing about three tons. It was related to the dugong and lamantine of the southern seas, and the *manatus* which occurs in Florida and along the Gulf coast. Its habitat seems to have been confined to the shores of the Commander Islands, where it was found in great numbers. Its flesh was very excellent food. Later it was eagerly sought after by the Siberian hunter, whose rapacity exterminated the whole species in less than a generation. The last specimen is said to have been killed in 1768, and hence museums have been very unsuccessful in procuring skeletons of the animal. In his "Voyage of the Vega," Nordenskjöld attempts to show that sea-cows were seen much later, even as late as 1854; but as he bases his assumption chiefly on the statements of some Aleutian natives, who, according to what Dr. Leonhard Stejneger recently has proved, confounded the sea-cow with a toothed whale (denticete), there seems to be no reason

* The correct name of this animal, Dr. Stejneger informs me, is *Rhytina gigas.*—TR.

whatever for modifying the results arrived at by Baer, Brandt, and Middendorff.*

Without this animal wealth it would have gone with Bering's expedition as it did later with the unfortunate La Pérouse, whose monument has found a place in Petropavlovsk by the side of Bering's. It would have been hopelessly lost on Bering Island. None of the participants would have seen Asia again, none would even have survived the winter 1741–42, for when the St. Peter stranded, there were on board only a few barrels of junk, a small quantity of groats, and some flour. The flour had been lying in leathern sacks for two years, and in the stranding had been saturated with turbid sea water, and hence was very unfit for food. How fatal, therefore, Waxel's and Khitroff's opposition to Bering might have been.

It was the night between the 5th and 6th of November that the St. Peter reached this coast. On the 6th the weather was calm and clear, but the crew were kept on board from weakness and work, and only Steller and Pleniser could go ashore with a few of the sick. They immediately betook themselves to examining the country, and walked along the coast on either side. Was this an island, or was it the mainland? Could they expect to find human assistance, and could they reach home by land? After two days of exploration, Steller succeeded in satisfying

* Dr. Stejneger says, after a very careful and exhaustive discussion of this question: "It may thus be regarded as fairly proved that the unknown cetacean, which in 1846 was observed near the southern end of Bering Island, was a female narwhal. But, whatever it may have been, one thing is absolutely sure: *it was not a sea-cow!*" For references see Note 65.—TR.

himself on these points, although it was nearly six
months before he definitely ascertained that the place
was an island.   Unlike Kamchatka, the country was
treeless, having only a few trailing willows of the
thickness of a finger.   The animals of the coast were
entirely new and strange, even to him, and showed
no fear whatever.   They had no sooner left the ship,
when they saw sea-otters, which they first supposed
to be bears or gluttons.   Arctic foxes flocked about
them in such numbers that they could strike down
three or four score of them in a couple of hours.
The most valuable fur-bearing animals stared at them
curiously, and along the coast Steller saw with won-
derment whole herds of sea-cows grazing on the luxuriant algæ of the strand.   Not only he had never seen
this animal before, but even his Kamchatkan Cossack
did not know it.   From this fact, Steller concluded
that the island must be uninhabited.   As the trend
of Kamchatka was not the same as that of the island,
and as the flora was nevertheless identical, and as he
moreover found a window frame of Russian workman-
ship that had been washed ashore, he was convinced
that the country must be a hitherto unknown island
in the vicinity of Kamchatka.

Bering shared this view, but the other officers still
clung to their illusions, and when Waxel, on the evening of the 6th, came ashore, he even spoke of sending a message for conveyance.   Steller, on the other
hand, began to make preparations for the winter.   In
the sand-banks, near an adjacent mountain stream, he
and his companions dug a pit and made a roof of

driftwood and articles of clothing. To cover up cracks
and crevices on the sides, they piled up the foxes they
had killed. He exerted himself to obtain wild fowl,
seal-beef, and vegetable nourishment for the sick, who
were gradually taken ashore and placed under sail
tents upon the beach. Their condition was terrible.
Some died on deck as soon as they were removed from
the close air of their berths, others in the boat as
they were being taken ashore, and still others on the
coast itself. All attempts at discipline were abandoned, and those that were well grouped themselves
into small companies, according to their own pleasure
and agreement. The sick and dying were seen on
every hand. Some complained of the cold, others of
hunger and thirst, and the majority of them were so
afflicted with scurvy that their gums, like a dark
brown sponge, grew over and entirely covered the teeth.
The dead, before they could be buried, were devoured
by foxes, which in countless numbers flocked about,
not even fearing to attack the sick.

More than a week elapsed before the last of the
sick were taken ashore. On November 10, the Commander was removed. He was well protected against
the influence of the outer air, and was laid for the
night under a tent on the strand. It snowed heavily.
Steller passed the evening with him and marveled at
his cheerfulness and his singular contentment. They
weighed the situation, and discussed the probability of
their whereabouts. Bering was no more inclined than
Steller to think that they had reached Kamchatka, or
that their ship could be saved. The next day he was

carried on a stretcher to the sand pits and placed in one of the huts by the side of Steller's. The few that were able to work sought to construct huts for all. Driftwood was collected, pits were dug and roofed, and provisions were brought from the ship. Steller was both cook and physician — the soul of the enterprise. On November 13, the barrack to be used as a hospital was completed, and thither the sick were immediately removed. But still the misery kept increasing. Steller had already given up all hopes of Bering's recovery. Waxel, who had been able to keep up as long as they were on the sea, now hovered between life and death. There was special anxiety on account of his low condition, as he was the only competent seaman that still had any influence, since Khitroff, by his hot and impetuous temper, had incurred the hatred of all. Moreover, those sent to reconnoiter, returned with the news that in a westerly direction they could find no connection with Kamchatka or discover the slightest trace of human habitation. It became stormy; for several days the boat could not venture out, and the ship, their only hope, lay very much exposed near a rocky shore. The anchor was not a very good one, and there was great danger that the vessel would be driven out to sea, or be dashed to pieces on the rocks. The ten or twelve able-bodied men that were left, being obliged to stand in icy water half a day at a time, soon gave way under such burdens. Sickness and want were on every hand. Despair stared them in the face, and not until November 25, when the vessel was driven

clear ashore and its keel buried deep in the sand, did
their condition seem more secure. They then went
quietly to work to prepare for the winter.

In December the whole crew was lodged in five underground huts (dug-outs) on the bank of the stream near
the place of landing.* The ship's provisions were divided
in such a way that every man daily received a pound of
flour and some groats, until the supply was exhausted.
But they had to depend principally upon the chase, and
subsisted almost exclusively upon the above mentioned
marine animals and a stranded whale. Each hut constituted a family with its own economical affairs, and daily

* These pits or earth huts lay in a direction from north to south. Next
to Steller's hut was the miserable pit in which Vitus Bering, a hundred
and forty-eight years ago, drew his last breath. August 30, 1882, Dr. Stejneger visited this place, of which he gives the following description in
Deutsche Geographische Blätter, 1885, pp. 265-6: "I was first attracted to the
ruins of the huts in which the shipwrecked crew passed a winter a hundred and forty-one years previous. On a projecting edge of the western
slope of the mountain, in the northern corner of the valley, stands a large
Greek cross. Tradition says that Bering was buried there. The present
cross is of recent date. The old one, erected by the Russian Company,
was shattered by a storm, but the stump may still be seen. No one thought
of erecting a new one, until Hr. von Grebnitski attended to the matter.
Directly southeast of the cross, close to the edge of a steep declivity,
about twenty feet high, lie the fairly well preserved ruins of the house.
The walls are of peat, about three feet high and three feet thick. They
were covered with a very luxuriant growth of grass, and, moreover, swarms
of mosquitoes helped make investigation very unpleasant work. * * *
The floor was covered with a thick turf, the removal of which was out of
the question. I probed the whole surface with a bayonet, but nothing of
significance was found. * * * A part of the crew were undoubtedly
lodged in the sandpits under the barrow, of which Steller speaks. And in
fact traces of the pits still exist, although they no longer have any definite form, being, moreover, so overgrown with vegetation that nothing
could be ascertained from them. Some Arctic foxes had burrowed there.
At our approach the whole brood came out, and in close proximity stood
curiously gazing at us. Steller and his companions are gone, but the
Arctic fox, which played them so many tricks, is still there. The pits,
now merely an irregular heap of sand filled with burrows, lie close to the
brook, where it curves sharply toward the west, cutting into the declivity
on which the house stands."—*Author's Note to American Edition.*

sent out one party to hunt and another to carry wood from the strand. In this way they succeeded in struggling through the winter, which on Bering Island is more characterized by raging snowstorms (poorgas) than severe cold.

Meanwhile, death made sad havoc among them. Before they reached Bering Island, their dead numbered twelve, the majority of whom died during the last days of the voyage. During the landing and immediately afterwards nine more were carried away. The next death did not occur until November 22. It was the excellent and worthy mate, the seventy-year-old Andreas Hesselberg, who had plowed the sea for fifty years, and whose advice, had it been heeded, would have saved the expedition. Then came no less than six deaths in rapid succession; and finally in December the Commander and another officer died. The last death occurred January 6, 1742. In all, thirty-one men out of seventy-seven died on this ill-starred expedition.

When Bering exerted his last powers to prevent the stranding of the St. Peter, he struggled for life. Before leaving Okhotsk he had contracted a malignant ague, which diminished his powers of resistance, and on the voyage to America scurvy was added to this. His sixty years of age, his heavy build, the trials and tribulations he had experienced, his subdued courage, and his disposition to quiet and inactivity, all tended to aggravate this disease; but he would nevertheless, says Steller, without doubt have recovered if he had gotten back to Avacha, where he could have obtained proper nourishment and enjoyed the comfort of a warm room. In a sandpit on the coast of Bering Island, his condition was hopeless.

For blubber, the only medicine at hand, he had an unconquerable loathing. Nor were the frightful sufferings he saw about him, his chagrin caused by the fate of the expedition, and his anxiety for the future of his men, at all calculated to check his disease. From hunger, cold, and grief he slowly pined away. "He was, so to speak, buried alive. The sand kept continually rolling down upon him from the sides of the pit and covered his feet. At first this was removed, but finally he asked that it might remain, as it furnished him with a little of the warmth he so sorely needed. Soon half of his body was under the sand, so that after his death, his comrades had to exhume him to give him a decent burial." He died on the 8th* of December, 1741, two hours before daybreak, from inflammation of the bowels.

"Sad as his death was," says Steller, "that intrepidity and seriousness with which he prepared to meet death was most worthy of admiration." He thanked God for having been his guide from youth, and for having given him success through life. He sought in every way possible to encourage his companions in misfortune to hopeful activity, and inspire them with faith in Providence and the future. Notwithstanding his conviction that they had been cast upon the shores of an unknown land, he was not disposed to discourage the others by expressing himself on this point. On the 9th of December his body was interred in the vicinity of the huts, between the graves of the second mate and the steward. At the departure from the island there was placed upon his grave a plain wooden cross, which

* Old Style.

also served to show that the island belonged to the
Russian crown. This cross was renewed several times,
and in the sixties, so far as is known, twenty-four men
erected a monument to his honor in the governor's garden
(the old churchyard) in Petropavlovsk, where a monument to the unfortunate La Pérouse is also found, and
where Cook's successor, Captain Clerke, found his last
resting place.

With Bering that mental power, which had been the
life of these great geographical expeditions and driven
them forward toward their goal, was gone. We have seen
how his plans were conceived ; how through long and
dreary years he struggled in Siberia to combine and exe-
cute plans and purposes which only under the greatest
difficulties could be combined and executed ; how by his
quiet and persistent activity he endeavored to bridge the
chasm between means and measures, between ability to
do and a will to do,—a condition typical of the Russian
society of that time. We have seen how he surmounted
the obstacles presented by a far-off and unwilling government, a severe climate, poor assistants, and an inexperienced force of men. We have accompanied him on his
last expedition, which seems like the closing scene of a
tragedy, and like this ends with the death of the hero.

He was torn away in the midst of his activity.
Through his enterprise a great continent was scientifically
explored, a vast Arctic coast, the longest in the world,
was charted, a new route to the western world was found,
and the way paved for Russian civilization beyond the
Pacific, while enormous sources of wealth — a Siberian
Eldorado—were opened on the Aleutian Islands for the

fur-hunter and adventurer. Russian authors have compared Bering with Columbus and Cook. He certainly
was for Russia, the land of his adoption, what the two
former were for Spain and England—a great discoverer,
an honest, hardy, and indefatigable pioneer for knowledge, science, and commerce. He led Europe's youngest marine out upon explorations that will ever stand
in history as glorious pages, and as living testimony
of what Northern perseverance is able to accomplish
even with most humble means.

And yet he only partly succeeded in accomplishing
what for sixteen years had been the object of his en-
deavors. His voyage to America was merely a reconnoitering expedition, which, in the following summer,
was to have been repeated with better equipments.

Chirikoff, who on the expedition in 1741, about
simultaneously with Bering,* discovered a more southerly

---

* Bancroft, who, strange to say, calls Chirikoff "the hero of this expedition," gives a detailed account of the voyage of the St. Paul after its separation from the St. Peter. Lauridsen does not do this, for the obvious reason
that he considers Chirikoff's expedition of but comparatively little importance, although he doubtless would be willing to second Bancroft's estimate
of Chirikoff as a man "who, amongst Russians, was the noblest and most
chivalrous of them all." There seems to be no reason to doubt that
Chirikoff sighted the coast of Northwest America about thirty-six hours
before Bering did. On the 11th of July signs of land were seen, and on the
15th land was sighted in latitude 55° 21′, according to Bancroft, who, at this
point in his narrative, exclaims: "Thus was the great discovery achieved."
Chirikoff's return voyage was fraught with hardships and suffering. Before
the expedition reached Avacha Bay, October 8, twenty-one were lost. The
pilot Yelagin alone of all the officers could appear on deck, and he finally
brought the ship into the harbor of Petropavlovsk. Croyère, the astronomer,
died as soon as he was exposed to the air on deck. Chirikoff, very ill, was
landed the same day. Eventful as the expedition in some respects was, it
nevertheless possesses no particular geographical or scientific interest, for
there is great doubt even as to where landings were made and what islands
were seen. Bancroft speaks very cautiously on these points. Sokoloff, however, declares emphatically that the land first discovered by Chirikoff was a

part of the North American coast, returned to Avacha in such an impaired condition that, in 1742, he could undertake no enterprise of importance.* On account of the great misfortunes that overwhelmed the expedition, Laptjef was prevented from completing the charting of Kamchatka. Thus we see that on every side of Bering's grave lay unfinished tasks. These tasks were inherited from the Dano-Russian explorer by his great successor Cook, and other younger navigators. Moreover, his death occurred at an extremely fatal period; for in these same dark December days while Bering was struggling with death in the sandpits of Bering Island, Biron, Münnich, and Ostermann lost their supremacy in St. Petersburg. The Old Russian party, the opponents of Peter the Great's efforts at reform, came into power,

slight projection of the coast between Capes Addington and Bartholomew of Vancouver's map. Moreover, the lands in these regions received no names from the St. Paul, whereas the St. Peter forged, along the islands of the North Pacific, a chain of names, many of which are still the permanent possession of geography. When it is furthermore remembered that Chirikoff was one of Bering's assistants, that the fitting out of the expedition was under the charge of Bering, and that upon him rested all responsibility to the government, it is certainly impossible for any fair-minded person to accept the statement that Chirikoff "must ever be regarded as the hero of this expedition." Bancroft does not, however, approve of Sokoloff's vainglorious expressions concerning "the achievements of Chirikoff, a true Russian, as against Bering the Dane." Principally in the one fact of a few hours' priority of discovery, Solokoff finds proof of "the superiority of the Russians in scientific navigation!" Bancroft occasionally reminds the reader that "Russian historians are perhaps a little inclined to magnify the faults of Bering the Dane," and in this instance administers to Sokoloff the following reproof: "So the learner is often apt to grow bold and impudent and despise the teacher. The great Peter was not above learning navigation from Bering the Dane." In speaking of Bering's death, Bancroft further retrieves himself—indeed, seems quite to supersede his former opinion— by saying: "Thus passed from earth, as nameless tens of thousands have done, the illustrious commander of the expeditions which had disclosed the separation of the two worlds and discovered north-westernmost America." See History of Alaska, p. 68 *et seq.*—Tr.

* Note 66.

and during Elizabeth's inert administration, all modern enterprises, the Northern Expedition among them, were allowed to die a natural death. At Avacha and Okhotsk affairs wore a sorrowful aspect. The forces of the expedition had been decimated by sickness and death, their supplies were nearly exhausted, their rigging and sails destroyed by wind and weather, the vessels more or less unseaworthy, and East Siberia drained and devastated by famine; only Bering's great powers of perseverance could have collected the vanishing forces for a last endeavor. On September 23, 1743, an imperial decree put an end to any further undertakings. Meanwhile, the crew of the St. Peter had, in August, 1742, returned to Avacha in a boat made from the timber of the stranded vessel. Chirikoff had previously departed for Okhotsk, to which place also Spangberg returned from his third voyage to Japan. Gradually the forces of the various expeditions gathered in Tomsk, where, first under the supervision of Spangberg and Chirikoff, and later that of Waxel and other officers, they remained until 1745. Thus ended the Great Northern Expedition.

But Bering's ill fate pursued him even after death. During the reign of Empress Elizabeth, nothing was done to make known the results of these great and expensive explorations, nor to establish the reputation of the discoverers. The reports of Bering and his coworkers, which make whole cartloads of manuscript, were buried in the archives of the Admiralty. Only now and then did a meager, and usually incorrect, account come to the knowledge of the world. Some of the

geographers of that day insisted that the Russian government system of suppression merely aimed at excluding the rest of Europe from that profitable maritime
trade through the Arctic seas for which the Northern
Expedition had opened the way. Ignorance on this subject was so great that Joseph de l'Isle ventured even
before the French Academy to refer to himself as the
originator of the expedition,—to rob Bering of his dearly
bought honor, and to proclaim to the world that Bering
accomplished no more on this expedition than his own
shipwreck and death. With Buache he published a book
and a map to prove his statements. The name De l'Isle
at that time carried with it such weight that he might
have succeeded in deceiving the world for a time, if G.
F. Müller had not, in an anonymous pamphlet written in
French, disproved these falsehoods. But even Müller's
sketch in *Sammlung Russischer Geschichte* (1758), the
first connected account published concerning these expeditions, has great defects, as we have seen, not only from
the standpoint of historical accuracy, but it also shows a
lack of appreciation of the geographical results obtained
by Bering.   Hence it would have been impossible for
Cook to render the discoverer long-deferred justice, if he
had not known D'Anville's map and Dr. Campbell's essay.
Thus it was West Europe that last century rescued
Bering's name from oblivion. In our day the Russian
Admiralty has had this vast archival material examined
and partly published, but much must yet be done before
a detailed account can be given of the enterprises we have
attempted to sketch, or of the. man who was the soul of
them all. We hardly feel disposed, with Professor Von

Baer, to urge the erection of a monument in St. Petersburg, as a restitution for long forgetfulness, former misjudgment, and lack of appreciation. As Russia's first navigator and first great discoverer, he certainly has merited such a distinction. We shall, however, consider our task accomplished, if we have succeeded in giving in these pages a reliable account of the life and character of a man who deserves to be remembered, not only by that nation which must ever count Vitus Bering among her good and faithful sons, but also by the country that harvested the fruits of his labors.

BERING'S MONUMENT IN PETROPAVLOVSK.

(FROM WHYMPER.)

APPENDIX.

APPENDIX.

BERING'S REPORT TO THE ADMIRALTY FROM OKHOTSK,
DEC. 5, 1737.*

FROM the instructions forwarded to me by His Imperial Highness, I learn that the Imperial College of Admiralty is inclined to the opinion that the expedition is lingering along idly on account of my heedlessness. This arouses in me no little anxiety for fear that I may incur undeserved wrath; yet in this matter I await the will of his Imperial Highness and the most gracious resolution of the Imperial College. For although, from the time the expedition was put in my charge until the present time, I have faithfully and diligently sought as quickly as possible to build vessels, put out to sea, and begin the execution of my work proper, everything has suffered delay on account of unexpected obstacles over which I have had no control. Prior to our arrival in Yakutsk, not a single pood of provisions had been sent to Okhotsk for the crew there, not a single vessel had been built for transporting these provisions and supplies, and not a single magazine had been built at the stopping places on the Maya and Yudoma rivers. No laborers were to be had, and no arrangements whatsoever had

been made by the Siberian government officials, notwithstanding the fact that an imperial ukase had
ordered these things. We have done all this. We
built transports, demanded laborers from Yakutsk, and
with great difficulty brought our provisions in these
transports to Yudomskaya Krest, — yes, with superhuman efforts our command and these laborers — since
even upon my demand but very few were sent — also
brought the supplies at Yudomskaya Krest (12,000
poods of flour and rice) to Okhotsk. Moreover, at the
stopping place on the Maya, at the mouth of the
Yudoma, at the Cross, and on the Urak, we erected
magazines and dwellings for the forces, and also built
four winter-huts between Yudomskaya Krest and Urak
as places of refuge during the winter. Furthermore,
in accordance with our plans, we built, in 1736, at
the stopping place on the Urak, fifteen, and during
this year, 1737, sixty-five vessels on which to float
the provisions down the Urak. Of these, forty-two
are still at the place of construction, the remaining
thirty-seven having departed with provisions in 1735.
All of this has been done under my orders, not by
the government officials of Siberia.

In Yakutsk, where I was at that time staying, we
built two vessels, the boat Irkutsk and the sloop
Yakutsk, and in 1735 sent them out on the expeditions assigned to them. We took pains to provision
them well, and furthermore sent four barges to the
mouth of the Lena with additional provisions for
them. In 1736 the Yakutsk had the misfortune to
lose its chief, Lieut. Lassenius, and many of the

crew. Others were hopelessly ill, and hence, as I feared that the work assigned to this expedition would not be accomplished, I was obliged to man the vessel anew from Yakutsk. The sick were taken to Yakutsk to be nursed. I did all that was possible for them, and by the help of God they were saved. For these same two ships I sent, in 1736, from the provisions of my command, two lighters with provisions, and during the present year, 1737, I have likewise sent a boat to the mouth of the Lena, as the provisions sent in 1735 were nearly exhausted. But from the voivode in Yakutsk we received no support whatever. From this it is evident that my stay in Yakutsk was necessarily prolonged. Nor was it possible for me to go to Okhotsk with my men until I had sent some provisions ahead. Otherwise I should have taken the risk of starving them to death, putting an end to all hopes of accomplishing anything, and thus incurring a heavy responsibility. Some of my men remained in Yakutsk in charge of the affairs of the expedition there, and to forward provisions. Others remained at the Maya harbor, Yudomskaya Krest, and at the Urak landing, to guard the magazines and attend to the transportation of necessaries to Okhotsk, for it is not yet possible to feed so many at Okhotsk. The fact that the voivode in Yakutsk made such long delay in appointing commissioners to receive and send me supplies, prevented me from keeping my men together and availing myself of their assistance. As early as June 2, 1735, I demanded the appointment of three commissioners and such assistants as I thought neces-

sary, to be stationed along the route. The authorities
at Yakutsk did not comply until the present year,
1737, and then only after repeated demands on my
part. But if I had neglected to attend to these matters, and had hastened the departure to Okhotsk, the
voivode — in my absence — would have done nothing,
and it remains to be seen how the transportation to
Yudomskaya Krest will be attended to. * * * As
the difficulties with which we have had to contend are
very obvious, and although as a consequence the immediate starting out of the expedition is improbable, I
can, nevertheless, conscientiously say that I do not
see how I could have in a greater degree hastened the
work of the expedition, or how I could have intensi-
fied the zeal with which I have worked from the very
beginning. Through this report I therefore most hum-
bly seek at the hands of the Admiralty a considerate
judgment, and hope that it will show that matters
have not been delayed through my carelessness.

It is on account of these obstacles, together with
the fact that there was much work to be done in
Okhotsk, that I have been unable to prepare, in a
short time, the ships necessary for the voyage. My
command has had to work at Spangberg's ships, which
are now ready. But also in Okhotsk, on the "Cat"
(Koschka), where these vessels and packet-boats are
being built, everything was bare and desolate. There
was not a building there,— nowhere to stay. Trees
and grass do not grow there, and are not found in
the vicinity on account of the gravel. In spite of
the fact that the region is so barren, it is nevertheless

very well suited for ship-building. It is a good place for launching, for starting out, and as a harbor of refuge for these ships. There is, in fact, no better place on this coast. Hence, according to Spangberg's directions, a house was built on the "Cat" for the officers, and barracks and huts for the men. For these buildings our men hauled the clay, made the tiles, brought wood from a distance of three to four miles, and carried fresh water from a distance of about two miles; for although the Koschka is situated at the mouth of the Okhota, the water in the river is very salt on account of the tide-water. Moreover, we have built store-houses and a powder magazine. I enclose three diagrams, showing what has been done in the years 1735, 1736, and 1737. My men in Okhotsk are now preparing ship-biscuits for the voyages, and are floating the necessary timber for the boats twenty miles down the river. They burn the charcoal used in forging, and the necessary pitch must be prepared and brought from Kamchatka, as there is no pitch-pine in the vicinity of Okhotsk.

In addition to this we are obliged to make our own dog-sledges, and on these bring our provisions from Yudomskaya Krest to the Urak landing. There is, too, much other work in Okhotsk that must be done in preference to ship-building, for it is quite impossible to get anything in the way of food except the legal military provisions, consisting of flour and groats. I must state, in this connection, that in the summer some cattle are sent with the transports from Yakutsk. These are obtained at the regular price and are dis-

tributed among the crews; but on account of the
great distance, and the reluctance of the Yakuts to
sell to others than the yassak collectors, except when
in great need, the supply has been limited.
Notwithstanding the fact that the authorities at Okhotsk were directed to prepare fish for the expedition, I
found that nothing whatever had been done in this
regard; but, on the contrary, they monopolized the supplies of the Tunguses, who furnished my first expedition
with an abundance of fish, and upon whom I had de-
pended. For this reason we are forced to give the men
leave of absence in the summer, so that they may obtain
food by fishing, thus causing a loss of time and neglect
of the work of the expedition. Our force might be
divided into different parties, for shipbuilding, fishing,
and miscellaneous work, but we have not found it expedi-
ent to do this. Especially on account of the fact that
many have been assigned to the work of transportation,
there are not as many engaged in shipbuilding as necessary, or as was ordered by the Imperial College of Admiralty. Lack of sufficient provisions has prevented this.
Here in Okhotsk we have but a small number of laborers.
The rest, for whom there will be no provisions until in the
spring, we have sent to Yudomskaya Krest to bring provisions and other necessary supplies on dog-sledges to the
Urak landing, and to construct at this place twenty new
barges for use in the spring of 1738. New barges must be
built every year, for those that are floated down the Urak
can not be returned on account of the swiftness of the
current. They are, however, used for other purposes in
Okhotsk. It takes four men ten days to build a barge,

and four or five to man one. I most respectfully ask the
Imperial College of Admiralty to consider the number of
men employed at this work, and what they are accomplishing. All of this, too, is being done by my forces.
From the government officer in Okhotsk, Skornjakoff-
Pissarjeff, we have not, since the day of our arrival here
up to the present time, received the slightest assistance
in transportation, shipbuilding, or anything else whatsoever. Nor have we any hope of obtaining any such
assistance in the future. And even if we should demand
support from him, we would only have long and fruitless
negotiations with him, for while in Yakutsk, he sent me
a written notification (February 28, 1737), refusing to
assist in the transportation from Yudomskaya Krest to
Okhotsk.

In addition to the facts here adduced, together with
my earlier reports to the Imperial College of Admiralty,
wherein I have given an account of my efforts for the
progress of the enterprise and shown the impossibility of
an early consummation of the main object of my expedition, I appeal to the testimony of all the officers of my
command. All of which is respectfully submitted.

BERING, *Commander*.

NOTES.

1. List of Russian Naval Officers. St. Petersburg, 1882.—V. Berch: The First Russian Admirals.—Scheltema: *Rusland en de Nederlanden*, III., p. 287.—L. Daae: *Normænd og Danske i Rusland*.

As Berch hints that Bering had many enemies in the Department of the Marine, I have made inquiries on this point. Admiral Th. Wessalgo informs me that Berch's account is entirely without foundation. Bering demanded and got his discharge in 1724, because he was dissatisfied with the regulations governing promotions.

2. *Sammlung Russ. Geschichte*, III., p. 50.—P. Avril's Accounts of America, collected in Smolensk, 1686.—Vaugondie: *Memoires*, p. 4. *Les géographes des 16' et 17' siècles ont toujours pensé que la mer separait l'Asie de l'Amérique*.

See also a very interesting essay on the first Russian accounts of America: The Great Land, Bolshaia Zemlia, in the Memoirs of the Department of Hydrography (*Zapiski*), Vol. IX., p. 78.

The name Anian Strait has arisen through a misunderstanding of Marco Polo's book (lib. III., cap. 5). His Ania is no doubt the present Anam, but the Dutch cartographers thought that this land was in Northeast Asia, and called the strait that was said to separate the continents the Strait of Anian. The name appears for the first time on Gerh. Mercator's famous maritime chart of 1569.

Dr. Soph. Ruge: Fretum Aniam, Dresden, 1873, p. 13.

3. G. F. Müller, in *Schreiben eines Russ. Officiers von der Flotte*, p. 14, seeks to take to himself all the honor for our knowledge of Deshneff's journey, but this is not tenable. See *Beiträge zur Kenntniss des russischen Reiches*, XVI., 44. Bering did not collect his information concerning Deshneff in Kamchatka, but in Yakutsk, and referred Müller to this matter.

A. Strindberg: *P. J. v. Strahlenberg,* in the Swedish Society for Anthropology and Geography, 1879, No. 6.

4. V. Berch: The First Voyage of the Russians, pp. 2–5.

5. Bering's report to the Admiralty, in The First Voyage of the Russians, p. 14, together with his original account in *Description géographique, historique de l'empire de la Chine. Par le Père J. B. Du Halde.* La Hague, 1736, IV., 562.

6. G. W. Steller: *Beschreibung v. dem Lande Kamtschatka.* Frankfurt, 1774.
Krasheninikoff: The History of Kamtschatka. Glocester, 1764.

7. A species of bears-foot, *Sphondylium foliolis pinnatifides.* Cleff.

8. Bering's fear of the Chukchees may seem in our day to put him in a bad light; but they who are familiar with the history of this people know that at the time of Bering they were very warlike. Both Schestakoff and Pavlutski fell in combat with them. *Neue nordische Beiträge,* I., 245.
J. Bulitsheff: *Reise in Ostsibirien.* Leipzig, 1858, p. 33.

9. The ship's journal, kept by Lieut. P. Chaplin, is the basis of this presentation. The first Voyage of the Russians, pp. 31–65. Von Baer has used it to some extent, but no other West European author.

In Bering Strait there are two Diomede islands. The boundary line between Russia and North America passes between them. The Russian island is called Ratmanoff or Imaklit, the American Krusenstern or Ingalisek. See W. H. Dall: Alaska, Boston, 1870, p. 249.

10. That Bering himself was the author, would seem to be shown by the fact that Weber who knew and associated with Bering, uses *verbatim* the same expressions concerning the first expedition. See Weber: *Das veränderte Russland,* III., 157.

11. Cook and King: Voyage to the Pacific Ocean, III., 244.— The only place where I have found any testimony to show that America was seen from the Gabriel is a chart by J. N. De l'Isle: " *Carte Générale des Découvertes de l'Admiral de Fonte,*" Paris, 1752, on which chart, opposite the Bering peninsula, a coast line is represented with the words: " *Terres vues par M. Spangberg en*

1728, frequentées à présent par les Russes, qui en apportent de très belles fourrures."

12. The Academy's map, 1737.—Müller's map, 1758.

13. See A. Th. v. Middendorff: *Reise in den Aeussersten Norden und Osten Sibiriens.*, IV., 56.

Concerning Bering's determinations of longitude and latitude, O. Peschel says: *Auf der ganzen Erde gibt es vielleicht keine wichtigere Ortsbestimmung, als die von Petropaulovski, insofern von ihr die mathematischen Längen in der Beringsstrasse abhängen, welche die Erdveste in zwei grosse Inseln trennt. Mit lebhafter Freude gewahrt man, dass schon der Entdecker Bering auf seiner ersten Fahrt trotz der Unvollkommenheit seiner Instrumente die Längen von Okhotsk, die Südspitze Kamchatkas und die Ostspitze Asiens, bis auf Bruchtheile eines Grades richtig bestimmte."—Geschichte der Erdkunde,* pp. 655–56.

A list of Bering's determinations is found in Harris's Collection of Voyages, II., 1021, London, 1748.

About the middle of the eighteenth century there was a violent attack on Bering's determinations. Samuel Engel, Vaugondie, and Bushing tried to show that according to these Asia had been put too far east. S. Engel: *Remarques sur la partie de la relation du voyage du Capt. Cook qui concerne le détroit entre l'Asie et l'Amérique.* Berne, 1781.—M. D. Vaugondie: *Mémoire sur les pays de l'Asie,* etc., Paris, 1774.—Bushing's Magazine, VIII., IX.

14. Cook and King: Voyage to the Pacific Ocean, III., 473: "In justice to the memory of Bering, I must say that he has delineated the coast very well, and fixed the latitude and longitude of the points better than could be expected from the methods he had to go by. This judgment is not formed from Mr. Müller's account of the voyage or the chart prefixed to his book, but from Dr. Campbell's account of it in his edition of Harris's Collection and a map thereto annexed, which is both more circumstantial and accurate than that of Mr. Müller." The chart which Cook refers to is a copy of Bering's own chart as given by D'Anville.

Concerning East Cape, Cook says: "I must conclude, as Bering did before me, that this is the most eastern point of Asia." p. 470.

15. See Steller's various works, especially the introduction to the one on Kamchatka, where it is stated that Bering returned "*ohne*

doch das geringste entdeckt zu haben." This introduction was written by J. B. S. (Scherer).

16. In Petermann's *Mittheilungen*, 1879, p. 163, Dr. Lindemann says that Bering turned back "without having seen, strange to say, either the Diomedes or the American coast." The author's authority is evidently W. H. Dall, an extremely unfortunate historian. The latter says: "Bering, naturally timid, hesitating, and indolent, determined to go no farther for fear of being frozen in, and returned through the Strait—strange to say—without seeing the Diomedes or the American coast." See Dall: Alaska and its Resources. Boston, 1870, p. 297.

17. *Geschichte der Entdeckungen im Norden*, p. 463.

18. C. C. Rafn: *Grönlands historiske Mindesmærker*. Copenhagen, 1838, III.

19. Hazii: *Karten von dem Russ. Reiche*, Nürnberg, 1788.— T. C. Lotter : *Carte géogr. de Siberie*, Augsburg.

20. Harris's Collection of Voyages, II., 1021, Note 34.

21. V. Berch: The First Voyage of the Russians.

22. *Beiträge zur Kenntniss des Russ. Reiches*, XVI.

23. The name appears earlier on the chart which accompanies Gmelin's *Reise durch Sibirien*, IV., 1752, and in Steller's *Reise von Kamtschatka nach Amerika*. But both of these authors must here be considered an echo of Müller.

24. See Müller's own review of the Russians' early knowledge of the peninsula in Vol. III. of *Sammlung Russ. Geschichte*. Even as late as 1762 the Cossacks could travel among the Chukchees only in disguise.—Pallas: *N. Nord. Beiträge*, I., 245.—During Billings's expedition hostilities were still smoldering.—East Cape is 600 miles from Anadyrskoi Ostrog.

25. J. D. Cochrane has, in Narrative of a Pedestrian Journey, London, 1825, App. p. 299, attempted to establish Pavlutski's route, unsuccessfully, however, we think. On the whole, accounts and opinions concerning Pavlutski are so uncertain, that it is impossible by means of the literature on this point, to give a final opinion. See Fr. Lütke: *Voyage autour du monde*, II., 238. "*Sauer dit que Pavlovtsky vint jusqu'au détroit de Bering; ce qui, au reste, n'est pas en lui même vraisenable.*"

26. Pallas: *N. Nord. Beiträge.* I. Chart.—Martin Sauer: An Account of Com. Billings's Geog. and Astr. Expedition. 1785-94. Chart.

27. M. Sauer: An Account, etc., p. 252, Note.—Fr. Lütke: *Voyage autour du monde,* II., 238. Note and chart: *Carte de la Baie de Sct. Croix. Levée par les emb. de la Corvette le Seniavine,* 1828, where the original Serdze Kamen is found in its proper place with the original Chukchee name, *Linglingay.*

28. Steller: *Beschreibung von dem Lande Kamtschatka,* p. 15. Steller sways back and forth between Müller's views and the account that he himself obtained of the real state of affairs. He met Müller in West Siberia in 1739, when the latter was filled with his supposed epoch-making discoveries in Yakutsk archives. In *Reise nach Amerika,* p. 6, Steller says: *"So verblieb es nichts desto weniger auf Seiten der damals gebrauchten Officiere bey einer kurzen Untersuchung des Landes Kamtschatka, von Lopatka bis zu dem sogenannten Serze Kamen, welche bey weitem das Tschuktschiske Vorgebirge noch nicht ist."* He has so little knowledge of Bering's work that he can immediately go on to say: *"Gwosdew ist viel weiter und bis 66 Grad Norderbreite gekommen."*

29. How varying the views on this subject have been even in the narrowest academical circles may be seen from the following: In a German edition of *Atlas Russicus,* 1745, Serdze Kamen appears as a mountain in the center of the Chukchee peninsula. (By Calque, placed at my disposal by A. Thornam, of St. Petersburg. In the French edition the name is not found at all.) On the maps which accompany J. E. Fischer's *Sibirische Geschichte,* 1768, and Gmelin's work, Serze Kamen and Kammenoie Serdze are found, but in different places of Bering Strait, both different from Müller's.

30. Cook and King: Voyage, etc., I., 469: "Thus far Bering proceeded in 1728, that is, to this head, which Müller says is called Serdze Kamen on account of a rock upon it shaped like a heart. But I conceive that Mr. Müller's knowledge of these parts is very imperfect. There are many elevated rocks upon this cape, and possibly some one or other of them may have the shape of a heart. "At four in the morning the cape, which, on the authority of Müller, we have called Serdze Kamen, bore S. S. West." III., 261.

31. Gvosdjeff's *Reise.* Note 121.

32. *Beiträge zur Kenntniss, etc.*, XVI., 44. Note.

33. Philip Johann Tabbert, ennobled in 1707 and called Von Strahlenberg, was born at Stralsund in 1676, and taken captive after the battle of Pultowa as captain in the army of Charles XII. He was banished to Tobolsk, traveled some years with Dr. Messerschmidt in Siberia, and together with other Swedish officers he made several maps of Siberia, which, without his knowledge or consent, were published in Holland by Bentinck, 1726, in *L'Histoire des Tartares*, etc., and reprinted in various works such as *La Russie asiatique, tirée de la Carte donnée par ordre du feu Czar.*" In 1730, Strahlenberg's own work appeared in Leipsic; it is marked by its minute knowledge of details. His representation of the Chukchees peninsula deserves attention as evidence of the knowledge the Cossacks had of this region, whereas there is nothing original in his representation of the coast-lines of Eastern Asia. Baer says that Strahlenberg's book and map was made by a Leipsic student, and that whatever it contains that is of value is taken from Messerschmidt. *Beiträge*, XVI., 126. Note 18.

34. This map is reproduced in Nordenskjöld's Voyage of the Vega.

35. Steller: *Reise von Kamtschatka*, etc., p. 6, where a very erroneous and unreasonable account of the result of Bering's first expedition is given.

36. Kiriloff's map is found in *Russici imperii Tab. Generalis et Specialis*, Vol. XLIII.

37. Strangely enough, no original copy seems to have remained in the archives of the Admiralty. Berch insists that no such copy exists. I investigated the matter in 1883, and later Mr. A. Thornam has examined the archives for this purpose, but without result.

38. Du Halde writes: *Ce Capitaine revint à Sct. Petersburg le premier jour de Mars de l'année 1730, et apporta une relation succinte de son voyage, avec la Carte qu'il en avoit dressée. Cette Carte fût envoyée au Sérénissime Roi de Pologne, comme une présent digne de son attention et de sa curiosité, et Sa Majesteté a bien voulu qu'elle me fût communiquée en me permettant d'en faire tel usage qu'il me plairot. J'ai cru que le Public me scauroit quelque gré de l'avoir ajoutée à toutes celles que je lui avois promises.*

In the Swedish geographical journal, "Ymer," 1884, there is an interesting account by E. W. Dahlgren of the copies of Bering's chart in Sweden.

39. Gmelin: *Reise durch Sibirien.* Introduction.

40. Bering's proposition was formulated as follows: (1) As the waves, according to my observation, are smaller east of Kamchatka [than in the open ocean], and, moreover, as I have on Karaginski Island found large fir-trees washed ashore, which do not grow in Kamchatka, it is my opinion that America or some intervening land can not be very far from Kamchatka (150–200 geographical miles). In case this is so, commercial relations with that country that would be to the advantage of the Russian empire could be established. This matter can be investigated, if a vessel is built of from 45 to 50 tons burden. (2) This vessel ought to be built at Kamchatka, as at this place more available timber is found than at other places [on the east coast]; moreover, provisions for the crew, fish and other animals are easily obtained. Besides, greater assistance can be obtained from the Kamchadales than from the inhabitants of Okhotsk. (3) It would not be without advantage to find out the sea-route from Okhotsk or Kamchatka to the mouth of the Amoor and farther on to the Japan Islands, as we there have hopes of finding inhabited regions. It would be well to establish commercial relations with them, especially with the Japanese, which promises the Russian empire no small advantage in the future. For this purpose a ship of the same size or a little smaller than the first might be built. (4) The expenses of this expedition in addition to the salaries and the materials, which could not be secured there, but would have to be taken along from here or Siberia, would, including the transport, amount to ten or twelve thousand rubles. (5) If it is considered advisable to chart the northern coast of Siberia, especially from the mouth of the Obi to the Yenisei and hence to the Lena, this can be done by sailing down these rivers or by expeditions by land, as these regions are under Russian rule.

VITUS BERING.

April 30, 1730.

These propositions were first published by Berch in "The First Russian Admirals," and later reprinted by Sokoloff in *Zapiski Hydrograficheskago Departamenta* (Journal of Hydr. Dept.), St. Petersburg, IX., Appendix.

41. Part II. is based upon the works of Von Baer, Middendorff, and Sokoloff.

42. General List of Russian Naval Officers, St. Petersburg, 1882.

43. *Zapiski*, IX., 250.—*Beiträge zur Kenntniss*, etc., Introduction.—Sokoloff: "Chirikoff's Voyage to-America," St. Petersburg, 1849.—Bering's wife was suspected of having acquired goods illegally, but there is no proof of this. When she, in the year 1738, returned from Siberia, the Senate, influenced by the numerous denunciations of her conduct, issued an ukase that her goods should be examined. At the inspection on the borders of Siberia it was found that she had a suspiciously large quantity of furs and other things. She rather overawed the authorities, however, and returned to St. Petersburg unmolested. Sokoloff gives no information as to whether the furs were illegally obtained or not. She was very much younger than Bering; in 1744, on making application for a widow's pension, she gave her age as 39 years.

44. The author is indebted to Admiral Th. Wessalgo for the following archival accounts.

The Admiralty to Captain Bering, Feb. 26, 1736.

Your expedition is a very protracted one, and apparently it is being conducted somewhat carelessly on your part, which is shown by the fact that it has taken nearly two years to reach Yakutsk. Moreover, it appears from your report that your stay in Yakutsk will be too long; in fact, there seems to be no reason to hope that you will succeed in getting any farther. As a consequence of all this the Admiralty is extremely dissatisfied with your arrangements, and will not let matters go on without an investigation. If in the future any negligence whatever occurs, an investigation will be instituted against you for insubordination to the decrees of His Imperial Highness and for negligence in an affair of state.

The Admiralty to Captain Bering, Jan. 31, 1737.

Inasmuch as you—in spite of the express orders of the Admiralty, wherein it is stated that your expedition is protracted and is carelessly conducted—have not reported to the Admiralty the cause of your delay, and say nothing about when you intend to leave Yakutsk, you are hereby deprived of your supplemental salary, and will receive only the regular salary, until you send such a report, and until you continue on the expedition which has been entrusted to you.

210 VITUS BERING.

The Admiralty to Captain Bering, Jan. 23, 1738.

From Captain Chirikoff there has been received by the Admiralty a report from Okhotsk with an accompanying copy of a proposition laid before you by Chirikoff, suggesting measures for a more speedy completion of the Kamchatka expedition under your charge. As no steps had been taken by you in this direction as late as May 8 of the same year, the Admiralty has concluded to demand an answer from you, if any plans have been made on the basis of Chirikoff's proposition, and if, contrary to our expectations, nothing has been done, we desire to know *why*,—since, according to the orders issued to you Feb. 21, 1737, you were instructed to show zeal and solicitude for the activity of the expedition, and that any neglect on your part would make you liable to the same punishment as that suffered by Lieutenants Muravjeff and Pauloff for negligence in conducting expeditions entrusted to them.*

(These officers were reduced to the rank of ordinary sailors.)

According to Bering's reports there were engaged in the Great Northern Expedition, excluding the Academists and the crew on the White Sea expedition, the following number of men:

	In the year 1737	1738	1739
From the Admiralty	259	254	256
From Siberia	324	320	320
Total	583	574	576

45. To an inquiry directed to the Russian Admiralty asking the reason for Bering's long stay in Yakutsk, Admiral Th. Wessalgo has given me the following information:

"In Yakutsk, which was the base of operations for the whole expedition, Bering was to secure wood, iron, and other materials for the building of the necessary ships, and, what is most important, he was to secure provisions, of which a yearly supply of 16,000 poods was necessary. Although the furnishing of provisions had been assigned to the Siberian authorities, they did nothing, in spite of urgent and repeated demands; hence Bering had to undertake this work himself. Moreover, the immense amount of materials and provisions collected here was to be sent to Okhotsk, a task which presented insurmountable obstacles: the country was a wild and

* The author gives extracts from other reports of the same tenor, which the translator has seen fit to omit, referring the reader for further information on this subject to Bering's own report, p. 195 of this volume.

desolate region, the local authorities refused their co-operation in promoting the enterprise, there was constant contention and disagreement among the various officers in charge, who were more concerned in their own personal interests than in the comman weal, and Bering himself—was a weak character."

46. Stuckenberg: *Hydrographie des russischen Reiches*, II.— Krasheninikoff: *Kamtschatka.*—Pallas: *N. Nord. Beiträge*, IV.— Sarycheff: *Reise*, etc.—*Zapiski*, etc.: IX., 331.—Schuyler: Peter the Great, II., 544.

47. On account of the Chukchee war, D. Laptjef was to go from Kolyma to Anadyr and from there send word to Bering for a vessel or to go himself to Kamchatka for it,—in either case he was to sail around the northeast point of Asia and reach the mouth of the Kolyma. When he, in 1741, arrived at Anadyr, Bering had departed for America, and hence he could do no more than build some boats, by means of which he, in 1742, charted the lower course of the Anadyr, and returned in 1743 to Yakutsk. *Zapiski*, etc.: IX., pp. 314-327.—*Beiträge*, XVI., pp. 121-122.

48. Baer says: *Es hätte dieser Expedition auch die volle Anerkennung nicht fehlen können, die man ihnen jetzt erst zollen muss, nachdem die verwandte Nordküste von Amerika nach vielfachen Versuchen noch immer nicht ganz bekannt worden ist. Auch hätten wir den Britten zeigen können, wie eine solche Küste aufgenommen werden muss, nämlich in kleinen Fahrzengen, zwar mit weniger Comfort, aber mit mehr Sicherheit des Erfolges.—Beiträge*, XVI., 123.

Middendorff: *Reise*, etc., IV., Part I., 49, says: *Mit gerechtem Stolze dürfen wir aber in Erinnerung rufen, dass zu seiner Zeit Russland im Osten des Nordens durch seine "Nordische Expedition" nicht minder Grosses vollbracht, als die Britten im Westen.*

Petermann's *Mittheilungen*, 1873, p. 11: *Der leitende Gedanke zur Aussendung jener Reihe grossartiger Expeditionen war der Wunsch * * * eine nordöstliche Durchfahrt zu entdecken.*

49. A. Stuxberg: *Nordöstpassagens Historie.* Stockholm, 1880.—Th. M. Fries: *Nordöstpassagen.* Nær og Fjærn, 1880, No. 417.

A. E. Nordenskjöld: The Voyage of the Vega.—In a long and favorable review of Nordenskjöld's book in *Beiträge zur Kenntniss*

des russ. Reiches, St. Petersburg, 1883, VI., 325, the Academist Fr.
Schmidt expresses himself in the following manner concerning
Nordenskjöld's presentation of the history of the Northeast passage:
*Die dritte Gruppe bilden endlich die russischen Reisen im Eismeer
und an den Küsten desselben, die ebenfalls ausführlich behandelt
werden. Hier fällt es uns nun auf, dass im Bestreben, jedem das
Seine zukommen zu lassen, die weniger bekannten Mitarbeiter an der
Erweiterung unsrer Kenntniss, denen wir gewiss ihre Verdienste
nicht absprechen wollen, fast möchte ich sagen auf Kosten unsrer
berühmten gelehrten Forscher hervorgezogen scheinen, von denen
namentlich Wrangell und auch Baer an mehreren Stellen Angriffe
zu erdulden haben, die wir nicht für gerechtfertigt halten können.
Auch Lütke * * * kommt sehr kurz weg.*
This criticism might be applied to other parts of Nordenskjöld's
historical writings.

50. St. Petersburg Academy's Memoirs (Bull. phys. math. Tom.
III., No. 10.)

51. *Beiträge,* etc., IX., 495. Baer says: *Es ist höchst erfreulich,
die mit schweren Opfern erkämpften Verdienste unserer Marine-
Officiere vom vorigen Jahrhundert von dem neuesten Reisenden in
vollem Maase anerkannt zu sehen.—Nach Herrn v. Middendorff ist
nun gerade Tscheljuskin der beharrlichste und genaueste unter den
Theilnehmern jener Expedition gewesen. Wir wollen ihn also gern
vollständig in integrum restituiren.*

52. *Zapiski,* etc., IX., 308. Chelyuskin's original account is
found in the same volume, pp. 61-65. The German translation
appears in Petermann's *Mittheilungen,* 1873, p. 11.

53. Cook and King: Voyage, etc., III., 391: "For the group of
islands, consisting of the Three Sisters, Kunashir and Zellany
(which in D'Anville's Atlas are placed in the track we had just
crossed) being, by this means, demonstratively removed from that
situation, an additional proof is obtained of their lying to the westward, where Spangberg actually places them, between the long. 142°
and 147°. But as this space is occupied, in the French charts, by
that part of the supposed Land of Jeso and Staten Island, Mr.
Müller's opinion becomes extremely probable that they are all the
same lands; and, as no reasons appear for doubting Spangberg's
accuracy, we have ventured in our general map to reinstate the

Three Sisters, Zellany and Kunashir, in their proper situation, and have entirely omitted the rest."—Cf. O. Peschel's account, p. 467, 2d Ed.

54. W. Coxe: An Account of the Russian Discoveries. London, 1781.

55. The pre-Bering explorations of Northwest America did not extend beyond the northern boundary of California, and had not succeeded in ascertaining a correct outline of the country. In the oldest maps of the new world, that of Ortelius (1570), Mercator (1585), Ramusio (1606), and W. Blaew (1635), California is represented as a peninsula; but on the maps of later cartographers as W. Samson (1659), Wischer (1660), J. Blaew, Jansen (1662), Fr. de Witt (1666), and Nic. Samson (1667), the country is represented as an island, and this view was held until G. de L'Isle (1720) adopted in his atlas the old cartography of the peninsula.

Gvosdjeff's expedition to Bering's Strait in 1732 is but slightly and very imperfectly known in West Europe. It was undertaken by Ivan Fedoroff, Moschkoff, who had accompanied Bering on his first expedition, and the surveyor Gvosdjeff. Fedoroff is thus the real discoverer of America from the east, and the world has given Gvosdjeff the honor simply for the reason that the reports of Fedoroff and his associate were lost and he himself died the year after. There is an interesting account of this enterprise in *Zapiski,* etc., IX., 78.

56. G. W. Steller: *Reise von Kamtschatka nach Amerika.* St. Petersburg, 1793.

57. R. Greenhow: History of Oregon, California and the Northwest Coast of North America, 3d ed., New York, 1845, p. 216.—W. H. Dall: Alaska and its Resources. Boston, 1870, p. 257.—Milet-Mureau: *Voyage de la Pérouse autour du Monde,* II., 142–144 and Note.—Vancouver: Voyage, etc.—Oltmann's: *Untersuchungen über die Geographie des neuen Continentes.* Paris, 1810, II.

58. A. J. v. Krusenstern: *Hydrographie,* etc., p. 226.—O. Peschel: *Geschichte der Erdkunde,* 2d ed., p. 463 and Note.

59. According to Wrangell, Dall and others, both Indians and Eskimos inhabit this region. Clans of the great Tinné tribe, Ugalenses, stay during the summer on the Atna River, and during

the winter on Kayak Island; but on the coast of the continent from
Ice Bay to the Atna River there are also found Innuits, the Ugalak-
muts.—See Vahl: Alaska, p. 39. The people that Bering found on
the island must, according to Sauer, have been Chugachees, Eskimos that live about Prince William's Sound.
        See also H. H. Bancroft, Native Races, San Francisco, 1882, Vol.
I.—Tr.

        60. Gavrila Sarycheff: *Achtjährige Reise im nordöstlichen
Sibirien, auf dem Eismeer und dem nordöstlichen Ocean.* Leipzig,
1806, II., 57.—Sauer: An Account, etc., p. 198. "This per-
fectly answers to Steller's account of the Cape St. Elias of Bering,
and is undoubtedly the very spot where Steller landed, and where
the things above mentioned were left in the cellar. Thus it is very
plain that Cape St. Elias is not the southern point of Montague
Island, but Kay's Island."—G. Shelikoff: *Erste und Zweite Reise.*
St. Petersburg, 1793.

        61. *Zapiski*, IX., 303.—The Coast and Geodetic Survey, 1882.
Maps.

        62. Dall: Alaska and its Resources, p. 300.—Vahl in his work
on Alaska repeats Dall's opinion in a somewhat milder form.

        63. Krusenstern: *Recueil de Mémoires Hydrogr.*, II., 72.—
Cook and King: Voyage, III., 384.—The Geodetic Coast Survey,
1882.

        64. Dr. Leonhard Stejneger, under date of June 9, 1889, writes
the translator: "The locality indicated in Lütke's map is correct.
It is consequently on the eastern side of the island.   Steller's statement that it was on the northern side is easily explained as follows:
The valley where he landed opens toward the northeast, and the
corresponding valley on the other side of the island runs southwest;
this side consequently became the southern side.   At the time of the
shipwreck the magnetic deviation was much more easterly than it is
now, so that *by compass* the direction of the eastern coast was much
more E.-W. than at present.   Throughout his description of
Bering Island, Steller says north and south, where we would say east
and west.

        "My visit to this locality in 1882, I have described in detail in
Deutsche Geographische Blätter (1885), where you will also find a
sketch map of it, as well as a plan of the house in which the survivors wintered.

"Since I wrote my account, I have been able to consult Steller's own description of the wintering, and I find that the house which I have described and given the plan of, was the one they built in the spring, after the freshet which drove them out of the dug-outs (*Gruben*) on the bank of the creek, traces of which are still visible. I also found a number of relics at a place which I took to be the point where they rebuilt the vessel. In a letter Mr. Lauridsen suggested to me the probability that I had found not this place, but the locality where the store-house was built, in which the men left what they could not carry on the new vessel, and that the latter must have been built near the southern end of the bay. After reading Steller's own account, however, I feel absolutely certain that the ship was built at the northern end, near the huts and dug-outs, at the place where I found the relics. It is quite probable, however, that the store-house was built in very close proximity, if not on the very spot."

65. Leonhard Stejneger: *Fra det yderste Osten*. Naturen, Vol. 8. Kristiania, 1884, pp. 65-69.—Proceedings of the United States National Museum, 1884. Investigations Relating to the Date of the Extermination of Steller's Sea-Cow, by Leonhard Stejneger.—Henry W. Elliott: A Monograph of the Seal Islands of Alaska, Washington, 1882.—*Neue N. Beiträge*, II., 279.—G. W. Steller: *Ausf. Beschreibung von sonderbaren Meerthieren.* Halle, 1753.—E. Reclus: *Geographie*, etc., VI., 794.

66. Concerning Chirikoff, full information is given in Sokoloff: Chirikoff's Voyage to America, St. Petersburg, 1849 (Russian). He died in 1748 at Moscow.

See also H. H. Bancroft, History of the Pacific States of North America, Vol. XXXIII., History of Alaska, San Francisco, 1886.— TR.

INDEX.

A

Academists, 70, 78; leave Tobolsk, 81.
Academy of Science, Russian, 57.
Addington, cape, 189.
Admiralty Bay, 145.
Admiralty, Russian, dissatisfaction with Bering, 95.
Afgonak, island, 156.
Aïno, 124.
Akischis, strait, 124.
Alaska, 178.
Aldan, river, 23.
Aleutian Islands, 134, 140; discovery of, 167, 187.
Aleutians, Nearer, 168.
Aliaska, 161.
Amassoff, 18.
Amchitka, 167.
America Pars, 14.
Anadyr, fort, 42.
Anadyr, river, Cossacks at, 16; the Gabriel at, 30.
Anadyrsk, 46.
Anian, strait, 13, 15.
Anjou, 110.
Anna Ivanovna, 63.
Apraxin, 9.
Archangel Michael, ship, 100.
Arctic Coast, charting of, 62, 83.
Arctic expeditions, 107.
Arctic explorations, work of Russia and England in, 3.
Arctic foxes, 181.
Arii Kamen, 175.
Asia and America, boundary between, 13.
Atka, island, 165.

Atna, estuary, 148.
Attu, island, 168.
Avacha, 127, 134, 170, 190.

B

Baikal, lake, 91.
Balshaya, river, 26.
Bancroft, H. H., note on, 64; 64; note from, 73, 140; note on identity of Kayak and St. Elias, 149; note on, 188.
Baranoff Cliff, 109.
Barants, map of, 14.
Bartholomew, cape, 189.
Bear Islands, 18, 67.
Bellini, map by, 20, 118.
Berch, V., authority, 41; opinion of Bering, 52, 61.
Bering Bay, 144; incorrect location of, 146.
Bering Island, 51; discovery of, 169; description of, 174.
Bering Haven, 149.
Bering Peninsula, 67.
Bering, Rivière de, 145.
Bering Strait, discovery of, 32; Gvosdjeff in, 130.
Bering, Vitus, first expedition, 2; nativity, 6; in Baltic fleet, 9; in Sea of Azov and Black Sea, 10; promotions, 10; in Archangel, 10; home of, 11; discharge and re-appointment of, 11; plans for first expedition, 12; knowledge of Siberian geography, 19; starts on first expedition, 21; at Irkutsk, 22; at Yakutsk, 22; in relation to

O

Obdorsk, 81.
Obi River, 21, 107.
Obi, gulf, 109.
Ofzyn, Lieut., 79; at Obdorsk, 81; in Gulf of Obi, 93, 109; saves the St. Peter, 171, 172.
Okhotsk, arrival at, 24, 62, 79; building of, 99; fleet in, 103.
Okhotsk, sea of, explorations in, 26.
Olenek, 34, 92.
Ostermann, 64, 73, 189.
Ostrog, Kamchatka, 27.
Otheres, 114.

P

Pallas, 45.
Patience, bay, 123.
Patience, cape, 54.
Patiloff, 21.
Pavlutski, Capt., 43, 45, 83.
Peschel, O., 117, 118, 146.
Petchora, 107.
Peter the Great, Scandinavians in service of, 7; death of, 21, 63.
Petroff, 96, 119.
Petermann, Dr., 111, 116.
Petropavlovsk, founding of, 127.
Pissarjeff, 65, 83; quarrel with Bering, 84; sketch of, 85, 95; removal of, 103, 126.
Plauting, 93–96, 135,
Plenisner, 153.
Pontanus, J. J., 14.
Popoff, Cossack, on Chuckchee peninsula, 17, 66.
Preobrashensky, bay, 31.
Pribyloff Islands, 178.
Prince William's Sound, 145, 148.
Pronchisheff, 81, 92, 93, 96, 109.

R

Reclus, 67.
Remesoff, atlas of, 16.
Ruge, Prof., 117, 119.
Russian fleet, founding of, 9.

S

Saghalin, island, 54; charting of, 125.
Sarycheff, Admiral, at Kuriles, 120; 146, 148.
Sauer, M., 146; description of St. Elias, 147.
Saunders, Vice-Admiral, 11.
Savjaloff, 167.
Schaep, H. C., 54.
Schelagskii, cape, 110.
Schelting, Lieut., 119.
Scurvy, 182.
Schwatka, 21.
Sea Cow, 179: correct scientific name, 179; extermination of, 179; importance of, 180.
Sea Lion, 178.
Sea Lion Island, 175.
Sea Otter, 177.
Seljonyi, island, 123.
Semichi Islands, 167.
Semidi Islands, 159.
Senate, Russian, orders of, 64.
Serdze Kamen, cape, 39 et seq.
Shafiroff, 85.
Shantar Islands, 65.
Shestakoff, 18, 56.
Shumagins, discovery of, 161; stay at, 162, 164.
Siberia, determinations of longitude in, 38; scientific exploration of, 68.
Sievers, Peter, 9.
Sikotan, island, 123.
Skeving, 9,
Skuradoff, 109.
Soimonoff, 73.
Sokoloff, K., 75; opinion of Spangberg, 84, 94; Bering's assistants, 95; opinion of Bering, 96, 100, 116; qualifications of, 137, 159, reproved by Bancroft, 189, note.
Spangberg, M., in first expedition, 21; at the Kut, 22; winter at the Yudoma, 24; sets sail, 26, 50; instructions to, 66, 77, 82; nativity of, 84; accusa-

tions against, 94, 96; at Okhotsk, 100; expedition to Japan,
102, 117; return to Bolsheretsk,
120; results of expedition, 125;
return to Yakutsk, 126; at
Kirinsk, 126; return from third
expedition to Japan, 190
Spangberg's Island, 123.
Staaten Eiland, 54, 117, 133.
St. Abraham Island, 168.
Stanovoi Mts., 84, 89.
St. Elias, island, 141 *et seq.*
Stejneger, L., Dr., translator's
preface; note on, 173, 178; note
by, 174; description of Steller's
Arch, 176; concerning sea-cow,
179, 180.
Steller, G. W., opinion of Bering's
first expedition, 46; 57, 92;
estimate of Bering, 97; at Okhotsk, 103; joins the Pacific
expedition, 135; nativity and
sketch of, 136; diary of, 137;
on American soil, 141; description of St. Elias, 147; 150;
ridicules Bering, 151; 165; description of animal life, 176;
honored by Stjeneger, 176, note;
care of the castaways, 181; account of Bering's death, 186.
Steller, Mount, 176, note.
Steller's Triumphal Arch, description of, 176, note; representation of, 177.
Sterlegoff, 80, 109.
St. Hermogenes, island, 152; discovery of, 156.
St. Johannes, island, 165.
St. Kresta Bay, 31; the Gabriel
at, 31, 46.
St. Lawrence Island, 34, 41.
St. Marcus Island, 167.
St. Paul, ship, building of, 100,
102; crew of, 135; course of, 139.
St. Peter, building of, 100, 102;
crew of, 135; journals of, 137;
course of, 139; return voyage,
156 *et seq.;* at Shumagins, 164;
determinations of latitude by,
167; stranding of, 172.

Strahlenberg, 18; outline maps
by, 20, 118.
St. Stephen, island, 158, 167.
St. Thaddeus, cape, 30.
Stuxberg, A., Dr., 111.
Suckling, cape, 146.

T

Tabbert (Strahlenberg), 55.
Taimyr, peninsula, 82, 93, 109;
cartography of, 114, 115.
Taroko, islands, 123.
Texeira, 55.
Three Sisters, islands, 124.
Tigil, 128.
Tobol, 79; launching of, 80.
Tobolsk, arrival at, 21.
Tolbukhin, Lieut., 102.
Tordenskjold, Peter, note on, 9.
Trane, Thure, 9.
Tumannoi Island, 158.
Tunguska River, 22.
Tuscarora, 139.

U

Udinsk, 62.
Ukamok, island, 158.
Urak, river, 23.
Ural Mts., 68.
Urup, island, 117.
Ustkutsk, 22.
Ust Maiskaya, 88.

V

Vancouver, 67, 144, 148.
Vancouver's Island, 158.
Van Dieman, 54.
Vangondie, R. de, 39.
Van Haven, 78.
Varkhoiansk, 102.
Vega expedition, 109, 113–115,
179.
Viligin, 18.
Vlaming, 112.
Volga, 80,
Von Baer, 36, 41, 48, 72, 98, 111,
115; concerning sea-cow, 180,
192.

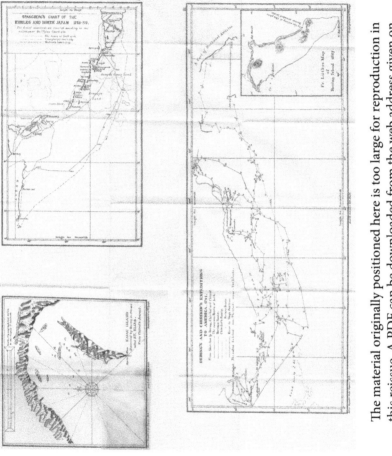

The material originally positioned here is too large for reproduction in this reissue. A PDF can be downloaded from the web address given on page iv of this book, by clicking on 'Resources Available'.

For EU product safety concerns, contact us at Calle de José Abascal, 56–1°,
28003 Madrid, Spain or eugpsr@cambridge.org.

www.ingramcontent.com/pod-product-compliance
Ingram Content Group UK Ltd.
Pitfield, Milton Keynes, MK11 3LW, UK
UKHW010339140625
459647UK00010B/704